An Ancient Syriac Translation of the Kur'an exhibiting New Verses and Variants

Analecta Gorgiana

639

Series Editor

George Anton Kiraz

Analecta Gorgiana is a collection of long essays and short monographs which are consistently cited by modern scholars but previously difficult to find because of their original appearance in obscure publications. Carefully selected by a team of scholars based on their relevance to modern scholarship, these essays can now be fully utilized by scholars and proudly owned by libraries.

An Ancient Syriac Translation of the Kur'an exhibiting New Verses and Variants

Alphonse Mingana

Kiraz

2012

Gorgias Press LLC, 954 River Road, Piscatav

www.gorgiaspress.com

G&C Kiraz is an imprint of Gorgias Press LLC

Originally published in

2012

ISBN 978-1-61719-588-4 **ISSN 1935-6854**

Extract from (1925)

Printed in the United States of America

AN ANCIENT SYRIAC TRANSLATION OF THE ḲUR'ĀN EXHIBITING NEW VERSES AND VARIANTS.

By A. MINGANA, D.D.

ASSISTANT-KEEPER OF MANUSCRIPTS IN THE JOHN RYLANDS LIBRARY AND SPECIAL LECTURER IN ARABIC IN THE UNIVERSITY OF MANCHESTER.

Foreword.

I.

AMONG the Syriac manuscripts brought recently from the East by the writer is one (numbered Mingana 89 and written about A.D. 1450) which contains controversial works against Jews, Nestorians, and Mohammedans by the West Syrian writer Barṣalībi, who died in A.D. 1171. The treatise against the Mohammedans is divided into three discourses (*maimrê*), subdivided into thirty chapters, two-thirds of which would offer no compensation for the trouble taken by a diligent reader intent on perusing them thoroughly. The last discourse, comprising chapters 25-30, is entirely composed of quotations from the Ḳur'ān, translated into Syriac. These the author adduces for purposes either of refutation or of illustration, and he divides his page in this part into two columns, the first of which contains the Ḳur'ānic quotations, and the second his own refutations or illustrations.

As the verses in the tract are often quoted without any introductory or editorial words, it is sometimes difficult to make out when a quotation ends and another begins. The aim of Barṣalībi in making use of these quotations is threefold: to confirm a given Christian doctrine, to draw attention to some apparent contradictions of the Ḳur'ān, and to put before his readers the story of some Biblical incidents as narrated in it.

Under the first head are all the Ḳur'ānic verses dealing with Jesus, His mother and His disciples, and with the Holy Spirit. The author often addresses in the second column the Christians or Mohammedans in some such phrases: "Examine what your (or: their, as the case may be) Prophet says about the Christ."

Under the second head fall all the passages in which the author puts side by side the apparently contradictory statements made by the Prophet. Here also the author addresses in the second column the Christians or the Mohammedans with some such words as: "Look how your (or, their) Prophet was inconsistent."

Under the third head occur all the passages dealing with the Patriarchs Abraham, Noah, and others whose history is often narrated in a different way from that found in the Canonical Books of the Old and New Testaments. Here also the author interpellates the Christians or the Mohammedans with words similar to those used under the first two heads. If we add to these the didactic passages quoted for the benefit of Christian readers, in the matter of the creation of man and the Universe, and of the life hereafter, we shall have a comprehensive synopsis of all the Ḳur'ānic citations, and a full abstract of the scope of Barṣalībi's work.

The Ḳur'ān in a Syriac garb greatly excited my curiosity and I began to peruse the above citations with some interest. I was not long in detecting the fact that they often represented a version which not only was not always in harmony with the *textus receptus* of the Ḳur'ān, but exhibited whole verses not found in it at all.

In 1914 when I edited some scraps of a palimpsest, the underwriting of which revealed scattered verses of the Ḳur'ān, I held to the traditional view, so ably maintained by Nöldeke in his classical *Geschichte des Qorāns*, that the sacred Book of Islam was collected and standardised on the initiative of the third Caliph by Zaid b. Thābit and other amanuenses.[1] In 1916, greatly under the influence of Prof. Casanova's investigations I contributed a monograph to the *Journal of the Manchester Egyptian and Oriental Society*,[2] in which I suggested that the traditional view on the compilation of the Ḳur'ān was not always satisfactory, and set forth the hypothesis that the Ḳur'ān, as we have it to-day, was finally standardised at a much

[1] *Leaves from three Ancient Ḳur'āns.* [2] Pp. 26-47.

later date, under the Umayyad Caliph 'Abd al-Malik b. Marwān. In the article *Qurān* in the late Dr. Hastings' *Encyclopædia of Religion and Ethics* (1918, pp. 547 sqq.), I endeavoured to add more weight to this theory.

Before proceeding any further with the Ḳur'ān itself, it will be useful to discuss the all-important question of the origin, provenance, and antiquity of its Syriac translation. Unhappily Barṣalībi throws no light on the subject. He begins his section as follows: "The third Discourse of the Treatise against the Muslims. Chapter 25, in which there are special parts of the Ḳur'ān in the upper column and a short refutation of them in the lower column, because a detailed refutation has been given in the previous chapters." The colophon of the whole work is by the author himself and runs thus: "Our Treatise against the Muslims has extended thus far. We have refuted their objection concerning the Trinity and the Incarnation of the Son, and by proofs taken from Nature and from philosophical books we have demonstrated our truth. Then we have confuted them in many points from their own book. After that we have arranged in one systematic division parts of the Ḳur'ān, which has been translated from their language into Syriac, and we have succinctly refuted it in the column that is below, because in the previous chapters we have given a detailed refutation. The time has now come to put an end to our labour. Let any one who reads and understands, profits and makes others profit, pray for Mar Dionysius the stranger, who is Jacob Barṣalībi from Milīṭīni, Metropolitan of Amed." Chapter 26 is entitled: "From the Ḳur'ān;" chapters 27-29 have no titles, and Chapter 30 is headed: "Further extracts from the Ḳur'ān."

It will be seen from the accompanying Syriac text of the colophon that the verb which we have rendered by "has been translated" with reference to the whole of the Ḳur'ān, may equally well be rendered by "have been translated" with reference to "parts" only of the Ḳur'ān.[1] We are not, therefore, in a position to infer with certitude from the above headings and colophon whether Barṣalībi had before him all the Ḳur'ān translated into Syriac, or only parts of it; but

[1] It would be in place here to remark that the Harvard MS. (see below) has an erroneous *wāw* after the verb (fol. 59b). This grammatical blunder does not deserve much attention as it cannot possibly be ascribed to Barṣalībi.

from the comprehensive list of all the translated passages given below we are inclined to adhere to the first alternative. The contrary hypothesis would drive us into endless surmises involving the existence of *Testimony Books* consisting of extracts and selections from the Ḳur'ān for the benefit of Christian controversialists. Of the existence of such books there is no trace of any kind in the history of the Syrian Churches. What seems to lend colour to our view is the fact that in the sentence following the one just reported (see the above colophon) the author clearly states that he has " succinctly refuted *it*," i.e. the whole Ḳur'ān and not only " parts " of it spoken of in the previous sentence.

If, as seems probable, there was great necessity for early Christians to possess a thorough knowledge of the religion of their new masters and neighbours, is it not more natural to suppose that they had a complete version of the Sacred Book of Islam, rather than merely short portions of it which at best would prove a great hindrance in their religious discussions ? We incline, therefore, to the belief that it is not intrinsically impossible to maintain the existence of a complete version of the Ḳur'ān in the hands of Christian doctors of the first centuries of the Hijrah. This hypothesis is rendered somewhat plausible by the fact that during the reign of some fanatical Caliphs unclean Christians could hardly even touch a Ḳur'ān in the presence of Muslims for purposes of reference ; and if all signs do not mislead us they would not be even allowed to possess officially Arabic Ḳur'āns in their private houses. In how many ancient copies of the Ḳur'ān do we not find in large characters, on the first page, the verses 76-80 of Sūrah LVI. which forbid even Muslims to touch it without having previously made their ablutions. (See Nīsābūri, *Gharāib*, xxvii., 113 ; edit. Cairo.)

The above remarks lead us naturally to the main point of our inquiry : when, where, and by whom was the Ḳur'ān translated into Syriac ? We must dwell at the outset on the fact that we do not deem it probable to suppose that Barṣalibi had any share in this translation. Any one who has read his Syriac works and noticed how careful he is to mention his name in sonorous phrases at the beginning or at the end of all of them, would hesitate to believe that if he had anything to do with the translation of the Ḳur'ānic pericopes under consideration, he would not have used the phrase " has been translated," but he would have written something like " which we Dionysius the stranger . . . have by the Grace of God translated from Arabic into Syriac."

Furthermore, in the second column where he refutes or illustrates the Ḳur'ānic verses, he sometimes upholds the traditional Muslim interpretation against the meaning of the Syriac text that he had transcribed in the first column. If he was both the author and the translator he could not have commented, in the way he did, on verses which did not square with the meaning he adopts in the Commentary. So, for instance, his refutation of verse 17 of Surah lxix. is in accordance with the Muslim traditional reading which implies that the throne of God was borne by eight angels,[1] while the Syriac lying before him, and which he quotes, clearly refers the "eight" to days and says that "they shall bear the throne of thy Lord on the eighth day." In the same way the text used by the author in his refutations found in the second column of verses v., 50, and lxi., 14, seems to be different from that found in the first column.

There is in this connection a linguistic phenomenon to which we wish to draw attention. When in lii., 20 the translator wishes to illustrate the Arabic *Sururin* which he had rightly rendered by *Piryāwātha*, he adds to it the explanatory Persian word *awkaith takhthā* "that is to say *couches*." If the translator was Barṣalībi—born and brought up in Malaṭya—he would not have used at Āmed a Persian word to explain a Syriac one. Does not this simple fact point to a time when Arabic had not yet supplanted Persian as a second language of the Christians of the Near East?

There is another linguistic feature worth mentioning. In the thirtieth chapter the author is evidently endeavouring to put side by side some apparently contradictory passages of the Ḳur'ān. This contradiction in terms, which he wishes to emphasise, is not always found in Arabic, but only in Syriac. If the author was working on an Arabic Ḳur'ān he would not have illustrated his point by wrong examples which did not prove his thesis. For instance, the Syriac verb ܛܥܐ means *to forget* (something), and the author finding it in his Syriac Version used of the forgetfulness of God rightly quotes it in this sense in connection with Ḳur'ān xxxii., 14, or xlv., 33, where the Arabic has نسي; but because he found this same Syriac verb in the Syriac version lying before him, he uses it in the form of

[1] Tabari, *Tafsīr*, xix., 37 (edit. Cairo). Zamakhshari, *Kashshāf*, ii., 1222 (edit. Calcutta). Baiḍāwi, *Anwār*, ii., 544 (edit. Bulak, 1296 A.H.).

ܛܥܝܐ ܠ which means "something escaping one's notice; hidden from one" answering to the Arabic خفي على in connection with iii., 4 etc., where it does not fit in with his assertion. This simultaneous use of the same Syriac word in two different connections could not have arisen from an Arabic Ḳur'ān. The argument will hold good even if verses such as xli., 53, and xxvii., 9, were alluded to by Barṣalībi. In xx., 54, the verb *yansa* is used of God as follows: "My Lord misleads not, nor forgets"; but the Ḳur'ān has "*my* Lord" while the Syriac has "*thy* Lord" with the addition of the word *nothing*, which is missing in the former; moreover it is the existence of the *lamadh* before the verb that is the deciding factor. The only difficulty is that in all our other references from the Ḳur'ān the word "God" is used instead of "thy Lord." In such verses as vi., 132 and xi., 123, *ghāfil* is in evidence.

We will here allude to a palæographically archaic feature which seems to ascribe to the tenth Christian century at the latest the *terminus ad quem* of the Arabic MS. of the Ḳur'ān from which our Syriac translation is derived, while the *terminus a quo* is lost in the mist of Ḳur'ānic antiquity: the first long quotation that the author gives from the Ḳur'ān embraces in a single whole, without any break in the text, all the first Sūrah and verses 1-10 of Sūrah ii. Now the second Sūrah is not introduced like the first by the ordinary formula: "In the name of Allah, the Compassionate, the Merciful," and although exhibiting the mysterious letters A.L.M. it is not preceded by its usual title and definition. We do not believe that any Arabic MS. of the Ḳur'ān lacked all these features after the tenth century, and if Barṣalībi—who in his Syriac writings may always be taken as a faithful repertory of ancient records—was not playing havoc with all literary decency, it was hardly possible for him to have been the translator of the Ḳur'ānic pericopes under consideration; cf. Ṭabari, *Tafsīr*, i., 35, etc. This refers only to the title and the description of the Sūrah; for the absence of the introductory formula see below p. 198.

Finally, the fact that the Syriac Version which the author quotes offers new verses not found in our Ḳur'āns, and various readings not mentioned by any Muslim commentator or reader, impedes us from ascribing it with any degree of probability to the time in which he lived, i.e. the twelfth Christian century. It is well known that the sacred

Book of Islam was finally fixed and standardised about three hundred years before this date. See also pages 214-215.

In this respect we know how careful were the Muslim theologians and *Ḳurrā'* in their reading and transcribing of the Ḳur'ān at the period of the 'Abbasid dynasty, that is to say from the time when we have positive proofs of the existence of a standard text. Controversies among *Ḳurrā'* have since then been confined to one or two vowels, one or two consonants, but hardly ever to complete phrases, despite the verses which some Shī'ah writers have invented to bolster up the political aim of the 'Alids.

That all the early *Ḳurrā'*, however, were not always a model of accuracy in the performance of their work is borne out by the answer that Iyās b. Mu'āwiah gave to the Umayyad Caliph 'Umar b. 'Abd al- 'Azīz (A.D. 717-720): "The *Ḳurrā'* are of two kinds: some of them do their work for the sake of the world to come, and these will not serve you; and some others do their work for the sake of this world, and on these you could not count."[1]

Islamic history has put on record cases of some doctors and *Ḳurrā'* who had different Ḳur'āns or knew verses of the Ḳur'ān not found in the official copies of the state. We will here mention Shanbūdh whose case became famous in Baghdād because he read and taught the Ḳur'ān "with disgraceful readings and anomalies which were an addition to the *muṣḥaf*[2] of 'Uthmān," and who in A.H. 323 was seized by the Sultan's emissaries and subjected to flogging.[3] Another instance is that of Ibn Ḳudaid (died A.H. 312) who had in his possession the Ḳur'ān of 'Uḳbah b. 'Āmir which was different in composition (*'ala ghair ta'līf*) from that of 'Uthmān.[4] Others who

[1] From *Baṣā'-ir al- Ḳudamā'* of Tawḥidi who died in A.D. 1009, fol. 191a of Arab. MS. 827 of the John Rylands Library. This work is rare, and I know only of one other copy preserved in Cambridge, No. 134 (p. 21 in Prof. Browne's *Hand-List* of 1900), cf. Brock, ii., 695. Our MS. is more fully described below, p. 202. On fol. 218a Tawḥīdi informs us that many anomalies in the reading of the Ḳur'ān were in very early times attributed to the considerable number of the non-Arab population whose conversion to Islam goes back to the time of 'Ali b. a Ṭālib. On fol. 264a a variant of transposition of words is recorded in Ḳur'ān L. 18, on the authority of the Caliph Abu Bakr himself.

[2] Exemplar or complete copy of the Ḳur'ān.

[3] Yāḳūt, *Irshād*, vi., 301-302 (edit. Margoliouth).

[4] R. Guest, in *Governors and Judges of Egypt*, by Kindi, p. 18.

ventured to register various readings had their books which contained them burned by order of the authorities.[1]

With Yāḳūt's account of the above unfortunate Doctor should be coupled the important statement of the author of the *Fihrist* who informs us (pp. 31-32) that Ibn Shanbūdh died in the court prison in 328, and gives us some astounding variants, additions, and verbal differences found in the Ḳur'ān that he was using.

Our present knowledge of various readings in the Ḳur'ān is mostly derived from the Commentators (chiefly Zamakhshari), from late books of *Ḳirā'āt* such as the *Muḳni'* of Dāni, and from stray quotations found in some early authors such as the *Mathālib*[2] of Ibn al- Kalbi and others, but these, as shown by the Ḳur'āns of Uḳbah b. 'Āmir and Ibn Shanbūdh, are not sufficient to enable us to form a clear opinion of the state of the sacred text in the time of its most critical period, which corresponds roughly with A.D. 660-710, and until some of those early works on the Ḳur'ān the existence—even if not the actual wording—of which was known to the author of the *Fihrist* (pp. 28-39) are recovered, or something tangible turns up from an unexpected quarter, we will only be able to formulate more or less consistent hypotheses, which however good can hardly stand as established facts.

The above cases belong to the fourth Islamic century. Before this time we know also of the early existence of the (now lost or purposely destroyed) Ḳur'āns of Ubayy b. Ka'b, 'Ali b. a. Ṭālib, Ibn Mas'ūd,[3] and of a few others, but is it likely that the Syriac translator would have chosen for the benefit of his co-religionists an unofficial and somewhat heretical text of which no Christian could make effective use in controversial discussions? What was there to tempt him in such an enterprise? Everything well considered we hold it, therefore, to be improbable that if a Syriac translation of the Ḳur'ān was in the hands of some Christian communities of the first centuries of the Hijrah, it

[1] Miskawaihi's *Experiences of Nations*, i., 285 (of the text).

[2] The information that the *Mathālib* contain Ḳur'ānic variants I owe to Mr. F. Krenkow, whose acquaintance with the scattered remnants of early Arabian poetry and prose is possibly unique.

[3] About Ibn Mas'ūd's Ḳur'ān we will recall the words of Diyārbakri (*Tārikh al-Khamīs*, edit. Cairo, 1302, i., 305): "If the Ḳur'ān of Ibn Mas'ūd had remained in the hands of the people, it would have caused a schism in the faith, on account of the disgraceful anomalies that it contained."

was not made from a text that was in every respect official and acknowledged by the bulk of the Muslim testimony of the time.

Researches in the domain of Syriac literature do not throw any important light on the point at issue. Most of the Syriac writers from the middle of the seventh century downwards appear on the whole to be well acquainted with the religion of their new masters, although in the historical sphere a few of them fall into grave errors in their biographical essays on the genealogy of the first Arab Caliphs and generals. From early times there have been, both in Syria and Mesopotamia, discussions between Christians and Muslims, a commendable enumeration of which can be found in Steinschneider's *Polem. u. apol. lit.* (1877), with Goldziher's continuation of it in *Z.D.M.G.* (33), and in our Ṭabari's *Book of Religion and Empire* (1922),[1] but to our knowledge in none of them is there mention of a Syriac translation of the Ḳur'ān. The first mention of the refutation of a complete Ḳur'ān recorded in Syriac literature is that undertaken by the East-Syrian writer Abū Nūḥ of Anbār, the secretary of the Muslim governor of Mosul, towards the end of the eighth Christian century, or about A.D. 790,[2] but since the work itself is lost we have no means for ascertaining the nature and the character of the sacred text that he used.

The above statement is subject, however, to an important qualification :

(*a*) From very early times Syriac writers, even those among them who knew no Arabic at all, referred to some statements made in the Ḳur'ān which it was very difficult for them to have discovered, unless they were either working direct upon a Syriac Ḳur'ān or upon first hand Christian anthorities versed in its knowledge. So, for instance, John of Phenek who was writing about A.D. 690 makes a clear mention of the fact that the Muslims had, from their leader Muḥammad, a special order in favour of the Christians and the monks.[3] This undoubtedly refers to Ḳur'ān v., 85. Now we cannot reasonably suppose that a monk living in the Bohtan district of Kurdistan, know-

[1] Some stress is laid on the importance of the controversial works of Abu Ḳurra in the *Century Supplement* of J.R.A.S., 1924, pp. 233 sqq.

[2] Assemani, *Biblioth. Orient.* iii., i., 212.

[3] John of Phenek, pp. 141 and 175 of my edition (*Sources Syriaques*, vol. ii., Leipzig, 1908).

ing no Arabic whatever, and writing purely for his fellow-monks, could have expressed himself on a delicate subject in such a confident way, if he had no Ḳur'ānic knowledge of any kind derived either from a translated Ḳur'ān or from some of his co-religionists versed in its doctrine.

(*b*) Many Syriac writers quote complete Syriac sentences of the Ḳur'ān in their controversial works written, like the present one of Barṣalībi, for the exclusive benefit of their co-religionists. Now the Syriac phraseology used by them in such quotations is sometimes identical with that which we are publishing in this study, so that we must either advance the not very probable hypothesis that this coincidence in phraseology is always due to a fortuitous encounter in the intricate linguistic peculiarities of the Arabic Ḳur'ān, or else resort to the more likely surmise that the Syriac controversialists were drawing upon a Syriac translation known to them. So, for instance, Barhebraeus quotes in his *menārath Ḳudhshê*[1] Ḳur'ān iv., 169; v., 77; and cxii., 1-4 in words very akin to those which we are editing to-day. Since it is unlikely that this very famous West Syrian writer was referring to the present work of Barṣalībi, is it not reasonable to suppose that these two writers were working upon a Syriac translation of the Ḳur'ān which they knew was coming down to them from the times that followed the first onrush of Muslim invasions and conquests?

In this respect it is not very gratifying to notice the way our inquiry is proceeding on negative lines, but history being a science based on facts and positive records, in the absence of them we can only grope our way in all directions in search of any opening which is capable of shedding a ray of light on a previously unexplored theme. If we were allowed to express an opinion on the subject we should say, but only provisionally and with extreme reserve (until fuller light dawns), that in view of the character of the present document, and on condition that all the indications of the author are scrupulously correct, the most propitious time for the appearance of such a Syriac translation of the Ḳur'ān as that which it appears to represent, would be the years of the reign of the Umayyad Caliph 'Abd al-Malik b. Marwān, some time between A.D. 684 to 704, before the final effort of the Caliphs

[1] Folios 53^b and 59^b of the Syriac MS. 61 of the John Rylands Library.

to fix a text bearing the authoritative stamp of the first Orthodox believers. To this period would also more appropriately point the Syriac word translated into Persian, which we have already examined, and the general phraseology of the translation which, although under Arabic influence (being a translation from Arabic), may nevertheless be considered good and moderately classical.

We will allude in this connection to the fact of the absence from Sūrah ii. of the introductory formula, "in the name of God, the Compassionate, the Merciful." This formula is certainly very ancient and, if I mistake not, is found in all the old MSS. of the Ḳur'ān that we possess—the oldest of which are by the way somewhat later than about the middle of the second century of the Hijrah, and correspond approximately with the first two decades that followed the 'Abbasid victory. Now unless we suppose, as we have already pointed out, that Barṣalībi was playing havoc with all literary decency, are we not allowed to argue from their absence that our Syriac translation was made from a Ḳur'ān in which the well-known formula was not, as at present, repeated before every Sūrah (with the exception of the ixth), but was found once only at the beginning of Sūrah i., i.e. the *Fātiḥah?* If the answer be in the affirmative, would it not be improbable to suppose that this formula was missing from the second Sūrah in any MS. of the Ḳur'ān written after the first century of the Hijrah? And if so, could not our Syriac translation also be ascribed to the end of the first Islamic century, or to the time of Ḥajjāj?

We may here add that we do not believe that Barṣalībi purposely omitted to quote the above formula, or that he had anything in view in so doing, because he actually quotes it before the first Sūrah and even gives us the three mysterious letters, beginning the second Sūrah, as the only break in the text between the two Sūrahs. See Nīsābūri's *Gharāib* (i., 76). That in the Ḳur'ān used by the author the first and second Sūrahs were considered as one is established by the fact that he (see p. 217) calls the second Sūrah as the first under the name of the *Cow*.

Of the same category of the apparently aimless omissions which might likewise tend to corroborate the point at issue is the refrain recurring after almost every verse of Sūrah lv.: "which of your Lord's bounties will ye deny," which is completely missing in Syriac. There are a few more textual phenomena of Ḳur'ānic phrases that are omitted in the translation. These the reader will easily notice for himself, and form his own judgment upon them without the aid of a Syriac scholar.

No one is more conscious than we are of the gravity of the above suggestion, as to the antiquity of the Syriac translation, and we hope that the care with which we have expressed ourselves will prove—as a Syriac saying has it—a healthy deterrent to any Arabic and Syriac scholar, whether Christian or Muslim, who might accuse us of lack of caution or of hasty conclusions. We are face to face with a Syriac text the character and the nature of which are not well defined. We have brought forward strong reasons for believing that it does not emanate from Barṣalībi, but we are not able to ascertain with confidence the exact time of its appearance. The question, therefore, of authorship, and all the subsidiary points attaching to it, should be left open until further evidence is available. We shall always be thankful to any scientific worker who is able to explain more fully and more satisfactorily than we have done the difficulties inherent in the Syriac translation as compared with the traditional *textus receptus* of the Ḳur'ān and the various indications of the MSS. After this remark we will proceed to enumerate the historical data that we have so far found in Arabic literature concerning the work of the standardisation of the Ḳur'ān that we firmly believe was undertaken by the Umayyad Caliph 'Abd al-Malik b. Marwān and his powerful lieutenant Ḥajjāj:

Kindi, who was writing some forty years before Bukhāri, outlines the history of the Ḳur'ān briefly as follows:[1] "Upon the Prophet's death, and at the instigation of the Jews, 'Ali refused to swear allegiance to Abu Bakr, but when he despaired of succeeding to the Caliphate, he presented himself before him, forty days (some say six months) after the Prophet's death. As he was swearing allegiance to him, he was asked, 'O father of Ḥasan, what hath delayed thee so long?' He answered, 'I was busy collecting the Book of God, for that the Prophet committed to my care.' The men present about Abu Bakr represented that there were scraps and pieces of the Ḳur'ān with them as well as with 'Ali; and then it was agreed to collect the whole from every

[1] *Risàlah* or "Apology," edit. Muir, pp. 70 sqq. Casanova in *Mohammed et la fin du monde*, 2ème fascicule, *Notes Complémentaires*, p. 119 writes: "Il faut, je crois, dans l'histoire critique du Coran, faire une place de premier ordre au Chrétien Kindite."

quarter together. So they collected various parts from the memory of individuals (as *Surat al Barā'ah*, which they wrote out at the dictation of a certain Arab from the desert), and other portions from different people; besides that which was copied out from tablets of stone, and palm leaves, and shoulder bones, and such like. It was not at first collected in a volume, but remained in separate leaves. Then the people fell to variance in their reading; some read according to the version of 'Ali, which they follow to the present day; some read according to the collection of which we have made mention; one party read according to the text of Ibn Mas'ūd, and another according to that of Ubayy b. Ka'b.

"When 'Uthmān came to power, and people everywhere differed in their reading, 'Ali sought grounds of accusation against him, compassing his death. One man would read a verse one way, and another man another way; and there was change and interpolation, some copies having more and some less. When this was represented to 'Uthmān, and the danger urged of division, strife, and apostacy, he thereupon caused to be collected together all the leaves and scraps that he could, together with the copy that was written out at the first. But they did not interfere with that which was in the hands of 'Ali, or of those who followed his reading. Ubayy was dead by this time; as for Ibn Mas'ūd, they demanded his exemplar, but he refused to give it up. Then they commanded Zaid b. Thābit, and with him 'Abdallah b. 'Abbās, to revise and correct the text, eliminating all that was corrupt; they were instructed, when they differed on any reading, word, or name, to follow the dialect of the Ḳuraish.

"When the recension was completed, four exemplars were written out in large text; one was sent to Maccah, and another to Madīnah; the third was despatched to Syria, and is to this day at Malaṭya;[1] the fourth was deposited in Kūfah. People say that this last copy is still extant at Kūfah, but this is not the case, for it was lost in the insurrection of Mukhtār (A.H. 67). The copy at Maccah remained there till the city was stormed by Abū Sarāyah (A.H. 200); he did not carry it away, but it is supposed to have been burned in the conflagration. The Madīnah exemplar was lost in the reign of terror, that is, in the days of Yazīd b. Mu'āwiah (A.H. 60-64).

[1] The birth-place of Barṣalībi.

"After what we have related above, 'Uthmān called in all the former leaves and copies, and destroyed them, threatening those who held any portion back; and so only some scattered remains, concealed here and there, survived. Ibn Mas'ūd, however, retained his exemplar in his own hands, and it was inherited by his posterity, as it is this day; and likewise the collection of 'Ali has descended in his family.

"Then followed the business of Ḥajjāj b. Yūsuf, who gathered together every single copy he could lay hold of, and caused to be omitted from the text a great many passages. Among these, they say, were verses revealed concerning the House of Umayyah with names of certain persons, and concerning the House of 'Abbās also with names.[1] Six copies of the text thus revised were distributed to Egypt, Syria, Madīnah, Maccah, Kūfah, and Baṣrah. After that he called in and destroyed all the preceding copies, even as 'Uthmān had done before him. The enmity subsisting between 'Ali and Abu Bakr, 'Umar and Uthmān is well known; now each of these entered in the text, whatever favoured his own claims, and left out what was otherwise. How then can we distinguish between the genuine and the counterfeit? and what about the losses caused by Ḥajjāj? The kind of faith that this tyrant held in other matters is well known; how can we make an arbiter as to the Book of God a man who never ceased to play into the hands of the Umayyads whenever he found opportunity? All that I have said is drawn from your own authorities, and no single argument has been advanced but what is based on evidence accepted by yourselves; in proof thereof we have the Ḳur'ān itself, which is a confused heap, with neither system nor order."

Barhebræus[2] has preserved the interesting and important tradition: "'Abd al-malik b. Marwān used to say, 'I fear death in the month of Ramaḍān—in it I was born, in it I was weaned, in it I have collected the Ḳur'ān (*Jama'tu*[3] *l'Ḳur'āna*), and in it I was elected Caliph.'" This is also reported by Jalāl ad-Dīn as-Suyūti,[4] as derived from Tha'ālibi.

[1] Cf. Nöldeke's *Gesch. des. Qorāns*, i., 255 (edit. Schwally).

[2] *Chron. Arab.*, p. 194 (edit. Beirut).

[3] Some writers endeavour to give to the verb *jama'a* the sense of "to learn by heart" (*Gesch. d. Qorāns*, ii., 6). If this meaning can be applied to the "collection" of 'Abdal-Malik and Hajjāj, why not also to the "collection" of 'Uthmān?

[4] *Tārikh al-Khulafā*, p. 227 (edit. Jarrett).

Maḳrīzi,[1] Ibn Duḳmāḳ,[2] and Ibn Ḥajar al-'As ḳalāni,[3] say about the Ḳur'ān of Asmā: "The reason why this Ḳur'ān was written is that Ḥajjāj b. Yūsuf Thaḳafi wrote Ḳur'āns and sent them to the head-provinces. One of them was sent to Egypt. 'Abd al-'Azīz b. Marwān, who was then governor of Egypt in the name of his brother 'Abd al-Malik, was irritated and said, 'How could he send a Ḳur'ān to a district of which I am the chief?'"

Ibn al-Athīr[4] relates that Ḥajjāj proscribed the Ḳur'ān according to the reading of Ibn Mas'ūd; and Ibn Khallikān[5] reports that owing to some orthographical difficulties such various readings had crept into the Ḳur'ān in the time of Ḥajjāj that he was obliged to ask some people to put an end to them.

The Arabic MS. of the John Rylands Library numbered 827[6] and dated (at the end of another work which precedes the one under consideration and which is written by the same hand) A.H. 732[7] A.D. 1331), contains an apparently unique work entitled: *Laḳāḥ al-Khawāṭir*: a collection of witty sayings, anecdotes, and traditions compiled by 'Abdallah b. Yaḥya b. 'Abdallah b. Muḥammad b. al-Mu'ammir b. Ja'far who lived in the sixth Islamic century, because he has dedicated his work to the 'Abbasid Caliph Mustaḍi (A.D. 1170-1180). On fol. 99ª of this MS. occurs the following anecdote: "And Rabī' b. Khaitham[8] was of the number of the great *Tābi'īn* and he had met with many of the *Ṣaḥābah* from whom he related traditions. The concubine of Rabī' b. Khaitham said that all the work of Rabī' was done in secret. If a man came to him while the exemplar of the Ḳur'ān (*muṣḥaf*) was open he would cover it with his mantle and begin to recite it aloud and say: "Until the

[1] *Khiṭaṭ*, ii., 454 (edit. Būlāḳ).

[2] *Intiṣār*, iv., 73 (edit. Būlak).

[3] *Raf'al-Iṣr* in Kindi's *Kitāb al-Umarā*, p. 315 (edit. Guest).

[4] iv., 463 (Tornberg).

[5] *Wafayāt*, i., 183 (text of Baron de Slane).

[6] This MS. was recently acquired by me in the East and was part of a collection where it was numbered: Mingana 122.

[7] This date is possibly that of the original from which the treatise was transcribed.

[8] Wrongly spelt "Khuthaim" in Ṭabari 3, 4, 2553. See about him, Ibn Rabban's *Book of Religion and Empire*, p. 72 (of my edition); Ibn Ḳutaibah's *Ma'ārif*, p. 36; Ibn Dur., p. 112; *Fihrist*, p. 225; Dhahabi's *Ṭabaḳāt*, p. 2 (edit. Wüstenfeld), etc.

reading of Ḥajjāj comes to us";[1] and if a noise was heard she (the concubine) was frightened."

We believe this to be a malicious allusion to the efforts made by Ḥajjāj for the standardisation of the Ḳur'ān, efforts of which Rabī' may or may not have approved.[2]

We will close all these quotations with a reference to an anecdote registered by Ṭabari,[3] in which Ḥajjāj is reported to have said in a speech that "Ibn Zubair had changed the Book of God"; whereupon Ibn 'Umar, who was drowsing from the effect of the length of the speech, rose and challenged Ḥajjāj, saying: "Neither thou nor he are able to do that." The answer that Ḥājjāj gave was: "It has come to my knowledge that thou shalt do it." And the story ends with the sentence: "But when he approached him privately, he was silent."

This traditional anecdote, worded as it is in a somewhat veiled style, does not clearly show what was in the mind of Ṭabari when recording it, but it does prove without any doubt that the name of Ḥajjāj was associated, in the mind of his contemporaries, with changes of some kind in the Ḳur'ān; this is all the more so because the anecdote is referred to in connection with Ḳur'ān x., 65, which asserts that the words of God do not brook any change.

[1] *wa yaḳūlu ila an ta'tiyana Kirā'at ul al-Ḥajjāji.* The MS. has corrections and additions on the margins by at least two different owners, and these words dealing with Ḥajjāj are by one of them and are as usual followed by a *saḥḥ*.

[2] It is useful here to remark that Tawḥīdi makes mention in his *Baṣā'ir* (*ibid.*, fol. 291a) of an unconclusive discussion which took place between learned *Kurrā'* before Ḥajjāj concerning the right reading and interpretation of Ḳur'ān viii., 17, and ends by deploring the fact that a beautiful saying of the Prophet has not found room in the sacred text, as if Ḥajjāj was responsible for the insertion into the text of the Ḳur'ān of this or that verse. On fol. 268b Tawḥīdi—to whom we actually owe a treatise on the art of writing (Brock, i., 244)—gives currency to an important and significant tradition to the effect that Ḥajjāj was the first man in Islam who wrote on papyrus: *awwal man Kataba fi l'Ḳarāṭīs*. The more I study Ḥajjāj the more I become convinced that he is one of the greatest men that Islam has ever produced. Was it not also in his time that Arabic coinage first came into use?

[3] *Tafsir*, xi., 96.

II.

The full list of the verses of the Ḳur'ān quoted in Syriac by Barṣalībi in the third discourse of his work is as follows : i., 1-7 ; ii., 1-10, 28, 29-35, 44-45, 81, 109, 130-131, 132, 139, 172, 254 ; iii., 2, 16, 18, 40-43, 45, 48-50, 52, 106, 109-110 ; iv., 50, 149, 154, 156-157, 162, 169 ; v., 16, 50-51, 69, 70, 72, 77, 85, 94, 109, 116 ; vi., 59, 76-78, 109 ; vii., 15-17, 171-172 ; ix., 34-35, 115 ; x., 94 ; xi., 9 ; xiii., 18 ; xv., 26-27, 39-43, 92-93 ; xvi., 104 ; xvii., 61, 87, 92-97 ; xix., 29, 34-35, 61-63 ; xx., 114-118 ; xxi., 52-65, 66-72, 91-92 ; xxii., 8-9 ; xxiii., 14, 103 ; xxiv., 2, 24 ; xxvi., 83-85 ; xxvii., 24 ; xxix., 13, 45 ; xxx., 7 ; xxxii., 14 ; xxxiii, 49-51 ; xxxiv., 3 ; xxxvi., 65 ; xxxvii., 14-15, 22-23, 97-113 ; xxxix., 32, 67, 74 ; xl., 78 ; xli., 8-11 ; xlii., 14 ; xlvi., 8 ; xlvii., 16-17 ; xlviii., 10 ; li., 47 ; lii., 19-21, 24 ; liii., 7-17 ; lv., 39, 46-56 ; lvi., 20-22 ; lvii., 4, 21-22, 24 ; lix., 7 ; lxix., 17 ; lxi., 14 ; lxvi., 12 ; lxxi., 14, 27-29 ; lxxii., 3, 26-28 ; lxxvi., 1, 16-20 ; lxxvii., 35 ; lxxxvi., 5, 16-20 ; xc., 1-4 ; xcvi., 1-3 ; xcviii., 1-7 ; xcix., 7-8 ; cxii., 1-4.

Interspersed amongst the Ḳur'ānic passages referred to in the above list are certain verses which the author, according to his own indications, quotes as from the Ḳur'ān, which he genuinely believes to be Ḳur'ānic, and which he treats in every respect as he treats the authentic verses of the Ḳur'ān, but which, on verification, prove not to be found in the Ḳur'ān of our days. Among them are some the origin of which cannot be traced to any other source but that of the Ḳur'ān. They appear to be Ḳur'ānic in the spirit and in the letter, and are not, and (with the possible exception of No. 1) even could not be, found in the tradition, to the taste of which they appear to be somewhat foreign ; at all events we have not been able to account for them through the channel of the *Ḥadīth*. They are the following, with the exclusion of the verse (in p. 230) which cannot be reconstructed except by a reference to two distinct Sūrahs, xi. 2, and xiii. 43 :

1°

"If all men gathered together from the East as far as the West to change one letter from the words of God, they will not be able to do it."

2°

"The Holy Spirit brought down from the Lord grace and light."[1]

[1] The author quotes also this verse as from the Ḳur'ān in Chapter xxiv. of the second discourse, but with the substitution of "*thy* Lord" for "*the* Lord."

3°

"No one understands the meaning of the Garden[1] except God."

4°

"He[2] is sitting on a throne."

The last verse needs some explanation. The word used for "throne" is *Kursya* which answers to the Arabic *Kursi*, and the nearest verse containing this word is ii., 256 which is, however, very remote in meaning, not having even a reference to "sitting." There are in the Syriac translation two other verses, xi., 9 and lvii., 4, which mention God's throne, but the Arabic word used in the Ḳur'ān for sitting is *istawa*, rendered into Syriac by *ittarraṣ*. The Arabic and the Syriac words are far from being the same thing as "sitting." Further, in the two passages mentioned above, the Arabic word for "throne" is *'Arsh*, rendered into Syriac by *'Arsa* which most generally means "bed, bier, and litter" and hardly ever "throne."

That the Ḳur'ān translated into Syriac had another verse in which the Arabic sentence used had *Kursi* and not *'Arsh* seems probable from the fact that Barṣalībi quotes two distinct Ḳur'ānic passages (see p. 218) in which it was stated that God's throne was upon water, in one of which he uses the word *Kursya* and in the other *'Arsa*, and he introduces the second by saying: "and in another place he (Muḥammad) wrote." As a matter of fact there is no other passage of the Ḳur'ān in which the throne of God is set up upon water.[3] The great imam Abu Ḥanīfah says in his *Waṣīyah* (fol. 12b of Arabic MS. 614 of the John Rylands Library) that this act of God making for and standing on the throne is to be believed as an article of faith, and he introduces it by the formula *nuḳirru*, "we profess."

There is another group of verses which it is useful here to examine. We are all aware of the fact that as the Gospels do not contain all the sayings of Christ, so the Ḳur'ān does not contain all the sayings of Muḥammad. Indeed Muslim tradition testifies to this in asserting that even the revealed passages are not consigned in their totality in the Ḳur'ān. Nöldeke[4] has long ago collected many such uncanonical

[1] Paradise of heaven; = Arab. *Jannah*. [2] God.
[3] Cf. Bukhāri, *Ṣaḥīḥ*, ix., 134 sq. (edit. Cairo, A.H. 1313).
[4] *Gesch. des Qorāns*, i., 234-262 (edit. Schwally).

passages which were scattered here and there in the tradition. In our present state of knowledge we are not in a position to affirm or to deny their existence in some early copies of the Ḳur'ān of the end of the first century of the Hijrah, but there seems to be a certain possibility in asserting that some ancient genuine sayings of the Prophet, now found only in the early tradition, might, in the heroic times of conquest, have constituted an integral part of some old Ḳur'āns.

Among the verses quoted by Barṣalībi as Ḳur'ānic there are some which, like those mentioned above, are not found in our traditional and official Ḳur'ān, but which are attested in the tradition to have been actually uttered by the Prophet. They are treated by the author as genuine and authentic, and said by him to have been excerpted, like the rest of the verses, from the Ḳur'ān that he was using. Since they are so treated by him, and since they are found in the first column of his work we will retain and consider them as such till fuller light dawns.

They are the following :

1° "And Adam was fashioned and was lying on the earth forty years without soul, and the angels passed by him and saw him."

This is in our days only a traditional saying and is reported by ancient and reliable authorities.[1]

Another verse of this category is the one relating to the creation of the pen before every other created thing ; and it is as follows :

2° "He first created the pen of the writer, and He said to the pen, 'Walk and write' ; and the pen answered, 'What shall I write ? and He said, 'Write concerning what happens till the end."

This is also reported by Ṭabari and others as a saying of the Prophet.[2] A special section is devoted to it in the *Waṣīyah* of the great imam Abu Ḥanīfah (fol. 20[a] in the Arabic MS. 614 of the John Rylands Library) where it is treated as an article of faith and introduced by the formula *nuḳirru*, "we profess." Cf. Muttaḳi's *Kanz*, ii., 449 (edit. Cairo).

Of the same kind is the following verse dealing with the creation of seven heavens and seven earths :

[1] Ṭabari, *Annales*, i., 89-90. Mas'ūdi, *Murūj*, i., 35 (edit. Bulāḳ), etc.

[2] *Annales*, i., 29-30. *Tafsīr*, xxix., 107. Ibn al-Athīr, *Kāmil*, i., 6-7 (Būlāḳ). Cf. Rāzi, *Mafātīḥ* (Cairo, 1278), vi., 330 ; Maḳdisi, *Baḍ'* (edit. Huart), i., 161.

3° " And seven heavens and seven earths were created like coverings one upon another."

A saying of the Prophet to this effect is also found in Ṭabari [1] and others.

There is another verse which is likewise treated by the author as Ḳur'ānic, but which has a pronounced traditional savour, and is undoubtedly traditional:

4° " My nation among Gentiles is like a white spot in a black ox."

The work entitled *Taysīr al-Wuṣūl ila jāmi' al-Uṣūl* of Wajīh ad-Dīn as-Shaibāni (edit. Cawnpore, ii., 163 in the chapter of *Faḍā'il*) contains the following saying of the Prophet: " You are among men like a black hair in a white ox, or like a white hair in a black ox." This is doubtless taken from Bukhāri (edit. Krehl, ii., 338).

At the end of all these uncanonical passages we will permit ourselves the observation that we do not believe that we have yet sufficient evidence to pronounce any verdict in favour of the view deduced from our Syriac authorities to the effect that the above traditional verses formed, at an unknown period preceding the time of Ḥajjāj, an integral part of some early copies of the Ḳur'ān. We are in complete ignorance both of the true state of the Ḳur'ān at that period, and of the exact provenance of the Syriac translation. In the present state of our knowledge, as we have already ventured to remark, we must follow the indications of the MSS. and look to the future for final results, in keeping constantly in our mind the important fact that we are dealing on the one hand with a sacred text, which, at least from the middle of the eighth Christian century downwards, can with great justice lay claim to an uncontestable traditional authenticity, and on the other hand with a Metropolitan of high integrity and unquestionable erudition and scholarship, who could not possibly have, or have been, deceived in a way that was as futile as it was stupid.

We will now discuss very briefly *some* of the variants in the genuine text of the Ḳur'ān. For the sake of conciseness we will divide them into two categories: (*a*) those which arise from Arabic words, mostly Ḳur'ānic, the nature of which may to a certain extent be safely conjectured; (*b*) those that arise from an Arabic text, the nature of which we are not able to ascertain with any degree of

[1] *Annales*, i., 50.

probability. Both categories are sometimes found in one single sentence. We will illustrate each group of such variants with examples :

First Category.

In xcvi., 3-4, the Ḳur'ānic sentence : "Read, and thy Lord the most generous, who *taught* by the pen," are rendered by "Read by thy Lord the noble who *is versed* in the knowledge of the pen that writes." The second member of the sentence is reminiscent of عَلِم for علّم. The phrase "that writes" may be an explanatory addition on the part of the translator who wanted to stress the fact that the Syriac word *Ḳanya* which he uses is here to be understood in the sense of "pen" and not of that of any other various meanings that the Syriac vocable possesses. According to Zamakhshari (ii., 1621), Ibn Zubair's copy actually read : "Who taught *writing* by the pen."

In ii., 131, the Ḳur'ānic verse : "And if they turn back, then they are *in a schism*," is in Syriac "And if they turn back and do not accept, they are *damned*." This seems to denote a reading شقاء for شقاق. Cf. Ṭabari, *Tafsīr*, i., 444.

In xli., 9, the sentence of the Ḳur'ān which reads : "And he placed on the earth *firm mountains* above it, and blessed it, and apportioned therein its food in four days *alike* for those who ask" is translated thus : "And He made *administrators* on the earth, and He blessed it, and apportioned its food in four days, as an *answer* to those who asked (or : ask)." The first variant seems to represent the word روساء for رواسي, and the second the word سؤال for سواء.

In ii., 30, the verse of the Ḳur'ān which means : "No knowledge is ours, but what Thou *hast taught us*, Thou art the knowing, the wise," is found in Syriac as : "No knowledge is ours except *the knowledge* that Thou art the knowing and the wise." The word علّمتنا seems here to have stood as علْمنا.

In xcviii., 1-2, the Ḳur'ān says : "Those of the people of the Book and the idolaters who disbelieved did not *fall off* until there came to them the demonstration, an apostle from God reading *purified* sheets (or : rolls), in which are solid Books," while the Syriac translation is : "Those who disbelieved among the readers of the Books and the idolaters who say two, will not *come back* until a proof of apostleship from God comes to them, that we (or : he) should read the Sacred

Books in which are written *demonstrating* texts." In the last part of the verse the word مطهّرة seems to have been understood as مُظْهِرة. As to the beginning of the verse the word *munfakkīn* appears to have been understood with a meaning somewhat different from that given to it by commentators (see Zamakhshari, ii., 1624, etc.). The clause "who say two" is nowhere found in the Ḳur'ān, and doubtless refers to Manichœans and Magians.

In ii., 1 and 4, the sentences of the Ḳur'ān which mean: "A *guidance* to the pious" and: "These are on *guidance* from their Lord," are rendered into Syriac by "A *guide* to the truthful" and: "These are on the *guide* from their Lord." This implies reading هادى for هدى. The translation refers the two phrases to the Ḳur'ān which is the actual guide.

In xxxvii., 101, the Ḳur'ān is: "O my boy, I have seen in a dream that I should sacrifice thee, *look then* what thou seest right," but the Syriac translation means: "O my boy, I saw in my dream that I should sacrifice thee, and *I vowed* what I saw." Here فانظر has evidently been فأنذِر.

In iii., 43 the Ḳur'ānic sentence which means: "And I will tell you what you eat and what you *store up* in your houses" is found in Syriac as: "And I will tell you what you eat and what you *talk about* in your houses." Probably تذكرون for تذخرون.

In xxvi., 84, the Ḳur'ān says: "And give me a tongue of truth *among the last ones*," but the Syriac translation is: "And give me a true tongue *in the end* (or: hereafter)." Probably الآخرة for الآخرين.

Second Category.

In ii., 131, the phrase of the Ḳur'ān: "but God will suffice thee against them" is found in Syriac as: "*But without pain and torment.* God will deliver thee from them." This seems to emanate from a totally different source.

In xcix., 8, the Ḳur'ān says: "And he who does the weight of an atom of good shall see it, and he who does the weight of an atom of evil *shall see it*." The Syriac reads for the last "shall see it" as follows: "*God shall see it*" which seems to denote a different text. Something of the restrictive meaning of the Syriac may be found in Ṭabari (*Tafsīr*, xxx., 173-175), who quotes authorities to the effect that only the unbeliever will see in the day of Resurrection the weight of an atom of evil.

In lxix., 17, the Ḳur'ānic : "Above them on that day *shall eight* bear the throne of thy Lord" is in Syriac written as : "They shall bear the throne of thy Lord above them *on the eighth day*." See about this p. 192.

In ii., 34, the Ḳur'ān says : "And you have an abode and a provision *for a time*," while the Syriac has : "And you have (on the earth) a dwelling *till the end of time*." Such a meaning has much in its favour. Zamakhshari (i., 70), distinctly states that the Ḳur'ānic *ila ḥīn* means "till the day of Resurrection" in other words, "till the end of time." The same thing is also asserted by Ṭabari (*Tafsīr*, i., 192).

In xv., 39-41, the sentence of the Ḳur'ān which reads : "I will make it seem seemly for them on earth, and I will seduce them all together, *save* such of Thy servants amongst them as are sincere . . .," is found in Syriac as : "I will lead them in the bad way, and I will seduce them all *even* Thy chosen servants . . . and He said, 'The right way is that Thou shouldst have no power over my servants'."

In lxxi., 28, the sentence of the Ḳur'ān which is generally understood to mean : "And they will only bear for children such as are voluptuous and unbelievers" reads in Syriac : "And of the voluptuous and licentious only unbelievers are born."

In lxi., 14, the Ḳur'ān says : "O ye who have believed, be ye the helpers of God," while the Syriac is : "O ye who have believed, be ye the Nazarenes of God, *the disciples of God*." The last sentence is not found in the Ḳur'ān and, if not an interpolation, seems to emanate from a source different from our Ḳur'ān of to-day. The translation in this verse of the word *anṣār* by *naṣrāyé* which generally means "Nazarenes" is curious. In other passages (iii., 45, etc.) the word is translated by *m'addrāné* "helpers."

To these two categories of variants we may add a third one, and that is the possible over-emphasising by the Syrian translator of the meaning of the Ḳur'ānic passages referring to Christians. In this connection, however, we are completely in the dark, and anything new we may advance should be taken as purely conjectural. We have indeed no reason to question the fairness of the translator, who, as every one may remark for himself, is endeavouring to give as accurate and faithful a rendering of the sacred text as could possibly be given by any ancient *Ḳāri.* What seems to establish his impartiality is his confidence that he is writing a work which is in every respect genuine, and his ignorance of the fact that what he is doing is in reality in conflict with the traditional interpretation of the *Ḳurrā'*. Indeed in none of the following verses is the author drawing any hostile conclusion in the second column from Ḳur'ānic premises enunciated in the first column.

Following this preliminary remark we may include under this head the fact that in verses where Moses and Jesus are mentioned simultaneously in a Ḳur'ānic verse, the latter invariably precedes the former. As the contrary is the case in the Ḳur'ān one may well ask the question : why has this anomaly occurred in the Syriac translation ? Is it possible to suppose that some early Ḳur'āns were worded in a way that violated the chronological order of events ? Is it not more likely to assume that this is due to the zeal of the Syrian translator for stressing the fact that Jesus is far greater than Moses ? But does this obvious chronological anomaly really help any Christian cause ? On the contrary, does it not weaken it in all directions ? One could hardly imagine a more stupid way of furthering a Christian cause, and I do not know any Syrian writer so dull witted as to resort to such ridiculous methods. The point, therefore, remains in the category of unsolved mysteries.

In the same category of mysteries is to be included the fact that the name of Jesus appears always in the translation as *'Īsa*, as it figures in the Arabic of the Ḳur'ān, and not *Īshō'*, as it is invariably written in Syriac ; and this in spite of the fact that the names of all the Patriarchs and Prophets of the Old Testament are given in the usual Syriac, and not in the Ḳur'ānic, form ; so we have *Mūshé* and not *Mūsa* (except in ii., 130, and xxx., 7) for Moses, *'Amram* and not *'Imrān* for his father, *Abrāham* and not *Ibrāhīm*, etc.

Another point which requires some explanation is the translation of xvi., 104, by : "The descent of the Holy Spirit is from thy Lord in truth to confirm the believers in Him." The Ḳur'ānic text of our days does not present any difficulty and reads : "The Holy Spirit brought it (the Ḳur'ān) from thy Lord. . . ." I consulted the commentators (Ṭabari, Zamakhshari, and Baiḍāwi), but found no variants for the beginning of the verse. Either, therefore, the Ḳur'ān lying before the translator read تنزيل for نزّله, or the translator himself deliberately read the word in this way, in order to refer the verse to the Holy Spirit instead of the Ḳur'ān. But could he really further his cause in the eyes of Muslims with such mistranslations, or rather blunders ?

A much more important verse for theological controversies is iv., 169. In the first half of it the Ḳur'ān has : " Believe then in God and in his *apostles*," but the Syriac translation reads : " Believe then in God and in His *Messiah*." Both readings are in conformity with the letter and the spirit of the Ḳur'ān, but the Syriac " Messiah " is more in harmony with this particular verse which deals with Christians and their Christ, to the exclusion of any other prophet or apostle. Is it possible that an ancient Ḳur'ān exhibited ومسيحه, for ورسله ? Is it not also possible to suppose that the important variant is due to a slip on the part of the translator in whose mind the Christian formula " God and His Messiah " may have been constantly vibrating ?

Another important passage is that dealing with the *Ḳiblah*, ii., 139. The Ḳur'ān reads : " Turn thy face towards the place of worship of holiness." All the commentators[1] understand the last words to mean the mosque of the Ka'bah, and Ṭabari[2] quotes ancient traditions to the effect that the precise direction towards which prayer is to be instituted is that of the door of the Ka'bah which, according to Burckhardt,[3] looks to the east. The Syriac translation of this passage actually reads : " Turn thy face towards the east of holiness." But we should perhaps be expecting too much from the ingenuity of the Syrian translator were we to assume that he knew the direction of the door of the Ka'bah and all the intricate Muslim questions affecting it.

The problem may be approached from another angle. Is it possible to suppose that a confusion has been made between the words المسجد and المشرق ? This should not look utterly impossible with old and undotted Kūfi Characters. Is it also possible to contend that the Christian translator wished to insinuate to his readers the fact that

[1] Ṭabari, *Tafsīr*, ii., 13. Zamakhshari, i., 114. Baiḍāwi (s.v.), etc.

[2] *Tafsīr*, *ibid.*, p. 15.

[3] See also Hughe's *Dictionary of Islām*, p. 256 sq. In Bukhāri (iv., 187 edit. Cairo), and others, Syria is on the left-hand side of the Ka'bah.

the Muslims also did turn, or had to turn, towards the east in their prayers, as the Eastern Christians did in that time?[1] If only we were justified in translating the Syriac word *Madhnḥa*, "east," by *Ḳiblah* more than half of the problem would be solved. It is probably along this line that the right solution of the problem is to be sought. In the preceding discourse the author has a whole chapter on *madhnḥa* in the sense of "direction of prayer," or something equivalent to *Ḳiblah.*

Before closing this short study it would be useful to remark that unfortunately the Syriac translation has not elucidated the meaning of some difficult words found in the Ḳur'ān. So the words used for the problematic *Houris* of paradise are simply transliterated as ܚܘ̈ܪܥܝܢ (with *siāmé*), and the words *Salsabīl* and *Zanjabīl* are quoted as *Salibasīl* and *Zanjibal* respectively. So is the case with *ḥanīf* (name of the traditional religion of Abraham in the Ḳur'ān), which is once translated by *Kashshīra*, "diligent," and once omitted in the translation of the first column but registered verbally in the refutation of the second column. The word *Ṣamad* occurs as *Ṣmīdha* and *Kāfūr* as *Kafru.*

We should also note the fact that the mysterious letters found at the beginning of Sūrah ii. appear also in the translation. As far as the names of Sūrahs are concerned only four are mentioned : ii., iv., v., xxix., and this mention, in the case of two of them, may even be due to the copyist who seemed to know something about Islam.

There are some passages in which there is clear proof of a double translation,—a phenomenon found more or less frequently in almost all translations. See for instance i., 5 ; ii., 2, 3, 5, etc.

An explanatory word resembling the case of a double translation is also found in iii., 109, and lii., 20. See also in this connection ii., 2, 7 and xcvi., 3-4. We have no means of ascertaining whether such words should be fathered on Barṣalībi or on the translation of the Ḳur'ān that he was using. See what has been said above concerning lii., 20.

In the following pages we will give a literal translation of the first column of all the third discourse of Barṣalībi, with the introductory

[1] If this were his intention it would indeed have been the depth of stupidity on his part. See a scathing saying of the Prophet concerning "the east" in Bukhāri, iv., 190 (edit. Cairo).

and editorial words, as found in the Syriac text which accompanies it. In this way the reader who is not familiar with Syriac will have before him every detail likely to enable him to form an independent judgment. Of the text of the second column, however, we give no translation because it is of little importance for the study of the Ḳur'ān, having been solely written for controversial purposes between Christians and Muslims ; but for the benefit of Syriac scholars we have deemed it advisable to give a facsimile of the Syriac text of all the third discourse of Barṣalībi containing both the first and the second columns.

Towards the middle of his discourse, the author, in order to illustrate the queerness of some Muslim beliefs concerning biblical events, has registered the fabulous story of an individual called 'Auṣ b. 'Anaḳ who was the only human being, apart from those sheltered in Noah's ark, who was not drowned in the Flood. The copyist, evidently to save space, or perhaps also by inadvertence, has written the first half of the story in the first column and the other half in the second column of the previous page (!) He noticed his error in time and corrected it.

This 'Auṣ b. 'Anaḳ is evidently 'Auj b. 'Anaḳ or A'naḳ spoken of by Ṭabari and others.[1] Barṣalībi's Christian authority seems to have been well acquainted with Islamic history, since he records about 'Auṣ the following saying : " No one remained from mankind except Noah and those who were with him in the ark, and 'Auṣ, son of 'Anaḳ, as the People of the Book say." This is an exact translation of a tradition reported by Ṭabari in the pages referred to above.

We say deliberately " Barṣalībi's Christian authority " because his own knowledge of Muslim religious and historical books seems to have been extremely meagre. Here is what he writes on this subject in the preliminary note of his third discourse (see facsimile) : " And 'Uthmān wrote this book (i.e. the Ḳur'ān), and it has been called the 'Uthmānic book. And the Muslims say that they have two other books apart from their Ḳur'ān : the book called *Maghāzi* in which are the deeds and the battles of Muḥammad. At the end of the other book which they call *Mukhtāra* they show the image of Muḥammad whom also they call Aḥmad." Of the innumerable Muslim works of *ḥadīth* and history, preceding the twelfth century, the author had apparently heard only

[1] *Annales*, i., 192 and 501. *Tafsīr*, xii., 23. Ibn al-Athīr, *Kāmil*, i., 35 (Bulāḳ).

of the *Maghāzi* and the *Mukhtāra* (!), and even these he had not seen and read; he was aware of their existence only by hearsay: "the Muslims say that they have. . . ."

A man of this calibre would hardly be able to translate the Ḳur'ān, or to use the early works of tradition in a controversial work between Christians and Muslims.

A reader has added on the margins some words or phrases of the Ḳur'ān in Garshūni, often in a perpendicular direction.

There are in the Syriac text some errors of the copyist to which we wish here to draw attention in the order in which they occur in the MS. We refer only to the text of the first column, and even there omit the slight grammatical mistakes, most of which are found more or less frequently in almost every Syriac MS.

ܠܥܪܒܬܐ	read	ܠܥܪܒܝ̈ܬܐ	(possibly)
ܘܪܟܬܐ	,,	ܒܪܟܬܐ	
ܩܪܝܡ	,,	ܟܪܝܡ	
ܢܟܪܘ	,,	ܢܟܪ	
ܕܐܟܘ̈ܟܘܢ	,,	ܘܐܟܘ̈ܟܘܢ	
ܠܢܠܝ̈ܡܬܐ (twice)	,,	ܠܢܠܩ̈ܬܐ	
ܕܡܕܢ	,,	ܕܡܕܡܬܐ	
ܫܠܡܬܐ	,,	ܫܠܡܬܗ	(possibly)
ܐܣܪ̈ܬܐ	,,	ܐܣܪ̈ܛܐ	
ܢܦܫܗܘܢ	,,	ܢܦܫܟܘܢ	(possibly)
ܘܠܡܗܟܠܘ	,,	ܘܠܡܫܟܠܘ	
ܕܡܬܚܘܝ	,,	ܕܡܬܚܪܝ	

ܢܬܠܒܒܘܢ	read	ܢܬܠܒܒܡ
ܬܝܡܢܬܐ	,,	ܕܝܡܝܢܬܐ
ܕܡܡܠܟ	,,	ܕܡܠܟ
ܕܪܘܚܐ	,,	ܕܪܘܚܐ
ܡܢܗ ܡܚܟܡ	,,	ܡܢܗ ܡܚܟܝܡ
ܠ	,,	ܠܝ
ܕܡܠܟ	,,	ܕܬܠܟ
ܕܐܡܪ	,,	ܕܐܡܪܬ
ܬܠܬܐ	,,	(?) ܕܬܠܬܐ
ܣܬܡܘ	,,	ܣܬܡ
ܘܠܐ	,,	ܐܠܐ

III.

Translation.

[*The italics denote the author's editorial words.*]

The third discourse of the Treatise against the Muslims. Chapter 25 *in which there are special parts of the Ḳur'ān in the upper column, and a short refutation of them in the lower column, because a detailed refution* (*of them*) *has been given in the previous chapters.*

In the name of God the merciful and the compassionate. Thanks to God, the lord of the worlds, the merciful and the compassionate, the King of the day of judgment. Thee we serve and thee we ask for help. Show us, and guide us in, the path of those on whom Thou hast lavished graces, and not of those Thou art wroth with, nor those who go astray (i., 1-7).

Alaph, Lām, Mīm. That book in which there is no doubt, a guide to the truthful. Those who believe in the thing that is hidden and unseen, and set up prayer, and from the victuals or rations that we gave, spend and feed; and who believe in what came down to, and was bestowed on, thee, and in what was revealed to those before thee, and believe in the hereafter. Those are on the guide[1] from their Lord, (and) these are who are the prosperous. But those who disbelieved, it is one and the same for them if ye warn them; and if ye advise them they will not believe. God has set a seal upon their heart and upon their hearing, and on their sight is dimness, and for them are grievous torments. And there are people who say 'we believe in God and in the day of judgment or trial,' but they are not believers. They deceive God and the believers, but they do not deceive except themselves, and they do not perceive and feel. In their heart is sickness, and God will make them still more sick. And they have grievous torments in what they lied. And when we said to them, 'Do not evil in the earth' they say 'It is we who do right things'" (ii., 1-10).

And then: "Those who disbelieved among the readers of the Books and the idolaters who say two,[2] will not come back until a proof of apostleship from God comes to them, that we[3] should read the sacred books in which are written texts which demonstrate. And the readers of the Books were not divided except after knowledge came to them. And they were not ordered to worship except God, in pure conscience, and to set up prayer and to give alms; and this is the true religion. But those of the readers of the Books who disbelieved and the idolaters are in hell for ever, and they are the most wretched of all the creatures. And those who believed and did good things, they are the best of all the creatures, and their reward from their Lord is the paradise of Eden" (xcviii., 1-7).

The "Surat al. Baḳarah" i.e. "cow" is the first book of theirs in which it is written thus: "Say 'We believed in God and in what came down to us and in what came down to Abraham, and Ishmael, and Isaac, and Jacob, and the Tribes, and what was brought to Jesus[4] and Moses and what was brought unto the prophets from their Lord.

[1] I.e. presumably the Ḳur'an of the beginning of the verse.
[2] I.e. Dualists (?) [3] Or: he.
[4] Written *'Īsa* and not *Ishō'*. Note his mention before Moses.

And we will not distinguish between them, and we are "mashlmāné"[1] to Him. And if they believe as you have believed in Him, they are guided, and if they turn back and do not accept, they are lost; but without pain and torment; God will deliver thee from them, for He is hearer and wise" (ii., 130-131).—"For each one of *the prophets* we have made a law and a different pathway, and had God pleased He would have made all of *them* one nation" (v., 52-53).

And when he wished to speak of the creation he said: "He first created the pen of the writer and he said to the pen, 'Walk and write,' and the pen answered, 'What shall I write,' and He said, 'Write concerning what happens till the end.'"[2]—"Read by the name of thy Lord who created man from a moist clay. Read by thy Lord, the noble, who is versed in the knowledge of the pen that writes"[3] (xcvi., 1-3).—"And seven heavens and seven earths were created like coverings one upon another."[4]—*And* "the earth was made in two days" (xli., 8).—"And His throne was upon the water" (xi., 9).

And in another place[5] *he wrote:* "He made the heavens and the earth in six days, and His throne was upon the water" (xi., 9).—"Say, 'Do you disbelieve in Him who made the earth in two days, and do you make partners to Him the Lord of the worlds!' And He made administrators on the earth, and He blessed it and apportioned its food in four days, as an answer to those who ask. Then He stretched in heaven which was but smoke; and He said to heaven and to earth 'Submit either willingly or forcibly'; and they answered Him 'We come having submitted.' And He decreed and ordered seven heavens in two days, and revealed in every heaven what was necessary to it" (xli., 8-11).—"It will not be what you will, but what God wills" (lxxvi., 30, and lxxxi., 29, etc.).

"And he who does the weight of an atom of good shall see it, and he who does the same of evil God shall see it" (xcix., 7-8).—*And in another place he said: God* "it is who created the heavens and the earth and all therein in six days, and then He stretched on the throne" (lvii., 4).—"And they shall bear the throne of thy Lord above them on the eighth day" (lxix., 17).

[1] I.e. *Muslims* = resigned. [2] See *Foreword.*
[3] This verse is taken from the second column.
[4] See *Foreword.* Cf. xli., 11.
[5] There is no other place in the Ḳur'ān. See *Foreword.*

CHAPTER 26.

From the Ḳur'ān.

"The Lord said to the angels, 'I am about to establish a vicegerent in the earth,' and the angels answered, 'Wilt thou establish therein one who will do evil therein, and shed blood therein, and we have glorified Thee, Confessed Thee, and hallowed Thee'" (ii., 28).—*And again he said:* "'I know what ye know not.' And He taught Adam all the names; then He showed the names to the angels and asked them, 'Declare to me these names if ye are truthful.' And the angels said, 'Glory be to Thee, no knowledge is ours except the knowledge that Thou art the knowing and the wise. And God said to Adam, 'Declare to them these names.' And God said to the angels, 'Did I not say to you that I know the secrets of the heavens and of the earth, and I know what you wish to say, and what is still in you before it is said?' And when we said to the angels, 'Adore Adam,' all adored him save only Satan, who refused and was too proud and became one of the unbelievers. And we said to Adam, 'Enter thou and thy wife into Paradise, and eat what you want and wish to eat; but do not draw near this tree or ye will be of the transgressors.' And Satan deceived them and drove them out, and we said to them, 'Go down together, one of you the enemy of the other, and in the earth there will be a dwelling for you till the end of the time'" (ii., 29-35).

"When we warned Adam from the beginning concerning the commandement, he forgot; and we did not find the warning in him. And when we said to the angels, 'Adore Adam,' they adored, save Satan, who became recalcitrant. And we said to Adam, 'Lo, he is a foe to thee and to thy wife. Take care that he should not drive you out of Paradise or thou wilt be wretched. And thou hast not to be hungry there, nor naked, nor thirsty; and thou wilt be in happiness (and immune) from heat and pain.' But Satan deceived him and beguiled him and said to him, 'I shall tell thee about the tree that it will be immortal, and a kingdom that shall not wane or perish'" (xx., 114-118).

And: "When thy Lord said to the angels, 'I am about to create a man out of clay; and when I have fashioned him, and breathed into him of my spirit, then fall ye down and adore him.' And all adored him, save Satan, and he became of the unbelievers" (xxxviii., 71-74).—"That future abode, we have made it for those who do not seek haughtiness nor do evil in this world" (xxviii., 83). —"'O Satan, what prevented thee from adoring whom I have fashioned with my hands? Hast thou been too big with pride, or hast thou been amongst the exalted?' Satan said, 'I am better, because Thou hast created me from fire, and him Thou hast fashioned from clay'" (xxxviii., 75-77).—"And when we created man from hard clay and from putrid mud" (xv., 26).

": And the spirits that dwell in the air,[1] which we have created before from sharp wind" (xv., 27).—"And Adam was fashioned, and was lying on the earth forty years without soul, and the angels passed by him and saw him."[2]—"A long time passed over the man, and there was nothing worth remembering about him" (lxxvi., 1).—*And Satan said:* "O Lord, because Thou hast deceived me I will direct them in the wrong way, and I will deceive them all, even Thy chosen servants; and He said, 'This is the right way that thou shouldst have no authority over my servants, save over those who follow thee of such as go astray; and hell is the trysting-place of all of them'" (xv., 39-43. Cf. xxxviii., 71-85).

": He said, 'For Thou hast deceived me, I will lie in wait for them in the straight path; then I will approach them from before their hands and from behind them, from their right and from their left, and Thou shalt not find many of them uttering thankfulness.' He said, 'Go forth therefrom, despised and expelled for those who follow thee; I will fill hell with you together'" (vii., 15-17).—"And Satan made their deeds and their work pleasing to them" (xxvii., 24; xxix., 37).—"And when we sent Noah to his people, he remained and was among them nine hundred and fifty years; and the deluge overtook them while they were unjust" (xxix., 13).

CHAPTER 27.

"And Noah said, 'My Lord, leave not upon the earth one of the unbelievers; if Thou shouldst leave them, they will lead astray Thy

[1] So the translator understood the *Jinns*. [2] See *Foreword*.

servants, and of the voluptuous and licentious only unbelievers are born. My Lord, pardon me and my father and my mother, and whomsoever enters my house believing, and (pardon) the believers men and women, and do not increase to the unjust except destruction'" (lxxi., 27-29).

"And Noah cried to his son who had gone aside, 'O my boy, come with us into the ark, and be not of the unbelievers,' and he said, 'I will climb a mountain and I will be saved from the water'; and Noah said, 'There is no one that can be saved from His command except the one on whom He may have mercy';[1] and the waters came between them" (xi., 44-45).—(*And he said of Noah's wife that she was of the unbelievers like the wife of Lot,*[2] *and that she was drowned in water because she did not go into the ark;*[3] *and also that one of Noah's sons did not go into the ark and was drowned.*[4] *And he further wrote:* "And if thou art in doubt of that which we *God* have sent down unto thee, ask those that were before you" (x., 94).—*He said:* "The Book has come down to thee in the justice and truth of that which was before it, and from the Torah and the Gospel; and the Torah and the Gospel were sent as guides to men" (iii., 2).

"What your Apostle orders you do (it), and what I order you not to do, desist from" (lix., 7).—"And when thy Lord took from the children of Adam, out of their loins, a grain for their children, and God made them bear witness against themselves and said, 'Am I not your God'? And they said, 'Yea, we bear witness,' lest you should say, 'Our fathers made partners to God, and we were but (their) children after them: wilt Thou then destroy us for what the vaindoers did'" (vii., 171-172).—"And when we took from the prophets their compact and their covenant, from thee and from Noah, and Abraham, and Jesus,[5] and Moses son of 'Amram, and took from them a rigid and truthful compact" (xxxiii., 7).

[1] Or: the one who loves him. [2] lxvi., 10.

[3] This is not found in the Ḳur'ān but is found in the Tradition possibly under the influence of lxvi., 10.

[4] xi., 45.

[5] In Syriac *'Īsa* (as above) and not *'Ishō'*. Note that here also Jesus precedes Moses.

CHAPTER 28.

"And when we showed Abraham all the heavenly Kingdoms and those of the earth that he should not be of those who doubt. But when the night fell on him and he saw a star he said, 'This is my Lord'; and after it had set he said, 'I love not those that go and come.' And when he saw the moon rising and shining he said, 'This is my Lord,' but when he saw it setting he said, 'If God does not become my guide I shall be of the people who err.' And when he saw again the sun rising from its place he said, 'This is my Lord, this is the greatest'; and after it had set he said, 'O people, I am clear of the partner that you are associating with God; I have turned my face to Him who commanded and created the heavens and the earth, and I am diligent to Him, and I am not of those who associate others with God'" (vi., 76-78).

"And when we bestowed on Abraham revelation before, we knew him. And he said to his father and to the people of his father, 'What is this image which you continually worship?' And they said, 'We found our fathers worshipping it.' He said to them, 'Both you and your fathers have been in an error that is obvious.' They said to him, 'Hast thou brought the truth to us, or art thou but of those who jest?' He said to them, 'Nay, but your Lord is Lord of the heavens and the earth and their maker; and I am one of the witnesses; and by God I will plot against[1] your idols that you took back from me. And he brake them all except the largest of the images, that they may not go back to it (or: him) and search (for it?). And the idolaters said, 'Who has done this with our gods? because he is of the evildoers.' They said, 'We heard a youth whom they remembered, Abraham by name.' They said, 'Bring him before the eyes of every man that they may haply bear witness.' They said to Abraham, 'Was it thou who did this to our gods, O Abraham? And Abraham answered them, 'It was the largest of them that did this to them, but ask them if they can answer.' The idolaters thought then in their mind and said, 'You are the wrongdoers of yourselves.' And then they bent their heads to the earth. And they said to Abraham, 'Thou knowest; are these able to speak? And Abraham answered and

[1] Doubtful meaning.

said to them, 'Will ye serve, beside God, what cannot profit you nor harm you? fie upon you and what ye serve beside God, while you do not see it.' And the idolaters got angry and said, 'Burn him and you will find your gods, if ye are going to do so.' And God said to the fire, 'Be thou cold in safety over Abraham, and wish him good.' And we contended for him, and we delivered Abraham and Lot to the land which we blessed for the worlds, and we bestowed upon Abraham, Isaac and Jacob, his grandson, and all of them we made righteous from the body" (xxi., 52-72).

"But after the time of the promise that his father made to him, and after it was made manifest to him that he was an enemy to God, he freed himself from him" (ix., 115).—"My Lord, grant me wisdom, and mix me with the righteous, and give me an honest tongue in the hereafter (or: in the end), and make me of the heirs of the Paradise of pleasures, and pardon my father who was of those who err" (xxvi., 83-85).—"I am going to my Lord, and He will guide me. O my Lord, grant me sons from the righteous; and we gave him glad tidings of a submissive boy. And when Abraham reached the spot, while walking he said to his son, 'O my boy, I have seen in my dream that I should sacrifice thee, and I vowed what I saw.' Then his son answered him, 'O my father, do what thou hast been bidden, and thou wilt find me, if God wills, one of the patient.'

"And when he made his son lie on his cheek upon his side we called, 'O Abraham, thou hast verified and fulfilled thy dream, and we are the rewarders of those who do good things; but if this deed were to be done, a great wrong would be done.' And we ransomed his son with a mighty sacrifice, and we left his son for him to the future generations. And peace be upon Abraham, for we have rewarded him with a reward that is due to the righteous; and he is one of our believing servants. And we gave him glad tidings of Isaac, a prophet from the righteous; and we blessed him and Isaac, and of their seeds is one who is righteous and one who is an obvious wronger of himself" (xxxvii., 97-113).

In Surat al-Baḳarah God said that: "We gave Moses the book and we followed him up with the prophets, and we gave Jesus,[1] son of Mary, the truth, and we fortified him with the Holy Spirit.

[1] In Syriac here also *'Īsa* and not *Īshō'*.

"O ye who have believed, be ye the Nazarenes of God, the disciples of God" (lxi., 14).—"And a party of the children of Israel believed, and a party did not believe; and we aided those who believed against their enemies, and when the morning came, they ruled over them" (lxi., 14).

And the angel said to Mary: "God gives thee the glad tidings of a Word from Him whose name is the Messiah Jesus,[1] son of Mary, living in this world and in the world to come; and he is of those who are near (to God). And he shall speak to people even when in the cradle, and in the assembly he is of the righteous. And Mary said, 'How can I have a son, when man has not touched me?' And he said to her, 'Thus God creates what He pleaseth; and when He decrees a thing He says: Be and it is; and He will teach him the Book, and the wisdom, and the Torah, and the Gospel; and he shall be an apostle to the children of Israel, and he shall say to them, 'I have brought to you a command from your Lord that I will create from clay something in the form of a bird, and I blow thereon, and it shall become a bird by God's command; and I will heal those affected with elephantiasis and the lepers; and I will bring the dead to life, by God's command; and I will tell you what you eat, and what you talk about in your houses. In these there is knowledge and miracle if ye be believers'" (iii., 40-43).

And God said to Jesus:[1] "I will make thee die and take thee up to me, and I will clear thee of those who disbelieved, and will make those who believed in thee and followed thee above those who disbelieved in thee, in the day of Resurrection. Then you will come to me, and I will decide between you concerning all that about which you disagreed. And as for those who disbelieved in thee, I will punish them with grievous and bitter punishment in this world and the next, and they shall have none to help them. But as for those who believed and did good things, He will pay them their reward, and God loves not the unjust" (iii., 48-50).

And in Sūrah of Women "Nisā'" the Jews say: "We have killed the Messiah, Jesus,[1] son of Mary, the apostle of God; but they did not kill him and they did not crucify him, but in appearance it appeared to them in this way. And those who differed in his story

[1] Here also *'Īsa.*

And when the prophets came to you, you were proud in your souls without pity, and some of them you killed and some of them you charged with lying" (ii., 81).—*The followers of Muḥammad said:* "We believed in God, and in what He revealed to us and in what He revealed to Abraham, to Ishmael, to Isaac, to Jacob, and to the Tribes, and in what was brought to Jesus [1] and to Moses, and in what was brought unto the prophets. We have not distinguished between any one of them, and we are faithful to them" (ii., 130).—"It is the baptism of God, and whose baptism is better than God's, and we worship Him" (ii., 132).

CHAPTER 29.

In the same "Cow" God said: "These apostles whom we sent, some of them are higher than the others; of them is one to whom God spake; but Jesus,[2] son of Mary, we gave him the knowledge of truth, and fortified him by the Holy Spirit" (ii., 254).—*In the "Table":* "And we announced to Abraham Jesus,[2] son of Mary, and we sent him after the prophets in order that he might confirm that which was given before him in the Torah; and we brought him the Gospel wherein there is the tradition of light, in order to confirm what was given before him in the Torah, and to guide and admonish the faithful" (v., 50).—*God said:* "O readers of the Books! Ye rest on nought until ye confirm the Torah and the Gospel, and all things given in them by their Lord" (v., 72).

And God said to Muḥammad that: "We sent many prophets before thee, the names of some of whom we have told thee, and of some of whom we have not told thee; and no prophet that I sent was ever able to work miracles except by my order; and when my order came, he decided with truth" (xl., 78).—*And Muḥammad said:* "I believed in every Book which has been given by God, and I am bidden to put straightness[3] between you; our God is your God. We have no argument with you, because to Him we will eventually go" (xlii., 14).—*Muḥammad said:* "I said nothing from the apostles, and I do not know what will be done with me or with you, and I am but a warner and a preacher" (xlvi., 8).—*And God said:*

[1] Here also it is spelt *Isa*, and it precedes Moses.
[2] Spelt '*Īsa*.
[3] Or: reconciliation.

are in doubt. But God took him up with Him, and God is mighty and wise. For there shall not be one of the holders of the Books but shall believe in him before he dies; and in the day of Resurrection he shall be a witness against them" (iv., 156-157).—"The Messiah, son of Mary, the apostle of God, the Word and Spirit from Him, and He sent it to Mary; believe then in God and in His Messiah" (iv., 169).—*Jesus*[1] *said:* "Peace be upon me the day I was born, and the day I die, and the day I shall be raised up alive." *And God said:* "The word of Jesus[1] is the word of truth concerning which[2] they dispute" (xix., 34-35).

"Those who repent and believe and act aright, these I shall admit into the Garden, and I shall not wrong them in anything; and they shall not hear there the voice of fear and fright, but that of joy and of peace; and they have therein their provision, morning and evening" (xix., 61-63).—*And God said that Mary:* "guarded her virginity, and we breathed into her[3] our spirit, and we made her and her son a sign unto the worlds. This is your religion and it is one religion, I am your Lord, and serve me" (xxi., 91-92).—*And God said:* "Mary, daughter of 'Amram, who guarded her virginity, and we breathed into her[3] our spirit, and she believed in God and in His Book, and became of the saints" (lxvi., 12).—*And God said to Muḥammad:* "The descent of the Holy Spirit is from thy Lord in truth, to confirm the believers in Him" (xvi., 104).—*And God said to Muḥammad:* "If they ask thee concerning the Spirit say to them, 'He is from my Lord, and I have been given but little from[4] His knowledge" (xvii., 87).

Chapter 30.

Further excerpts from the Ḳur'ān, from various places.

About whom who studies their book without knowledge he said thus: "Amongst men there is one who wrangles concerning God without knowledge or straightforwardness or an illuminating book; and he turned from that to stray away from the path of God;[5] for him there is disgrace in this world, and in that day of Resurrection we will

[1] Here also *'Īsa.* [2] Or: whom. [3] Or: it. [4] Or: of.
[5] Or: he turned from straying away from the path of God.

make him taste the torment of burning" (xxii., 8-9).—*And he said:* "Come to our word and yours which is (laid down) plainly, that we will serve God alone" (iii., 57).—"They disbelieve who say, 'God is Trinity'" (cf. v. 77).[1]—*And Muḥammad said:* "My nation among Gentiles is like a white spot in a black ox."[2]—*If they ask thee concerning signs,* "say to them, 'Signs are with God'" (vi., 109).—"Naught hindered us from sending signs, save that those of old said they were lies" (xvii., 61).

"And the unbelievers say 'Unless a sign come down upon him from his Lord.' Thou art nothing but a warner, and every nation has its guide" (xiii., 8).—"The *Ṣmīdha* is one; He begets not and He is not begotten, and there is no one similar or like unto Him" (cxii., 1-4).—"O prophet, we have made lawful (for thee) thy wives whose dowry thou hast given, and every thing that thy right hand possesses from what God has lavished on thee, and the daughters of thy paternal uncle and the daughters of thy paternal aunts, and the daughters of thy maternal uncle and the daughters of thy maternal aunts who fled[3] with thee, and any believing woman if she gives herself up exclusively to the Prophet, if the Prophet desires to approach her; she is given to thee in a special manner to the exclusion of all the believers. We know what we ordained for them concerning their wives and what their right hand possesses, that there should be no blame on thee; and God permits and forgives. Put off whomsoever thou wilt of them and take with thyself whomsoever thou wilt, and if thou desirest to take one of those thou hast divorced, thou wilt be without blame if thou takest her" (xxxiii., 49-51).

"Those who disbelieve in God and His apostles desire to make a distinction between God and His apostles and say, that they believe in part and disbelieve in part, and desire to take a midway course between this and that" (iv., 149).—"Had they maintained the Torah and the Gospel, what has come down to them from their Lord, they would have eaten from above their heads and from below their feet. Among them is a righteous nation, and the majority of them profess badly" (v., 70).—"Had the holders of the Books believed it would have been

[1] This verse is more exactly quoted below. Is it possible that there was another Kur'ānic verse worded in this way?

[2] See *Foreword.*

[3] Syriac: *hagrān* (from *hagar*).

better for them. There are believers among them, but the majority of them are wicked" (iii., 106).—"You pervert the words from their places" (iv., 48; v., 16).—*Jesus said:* "Who will be my helper with God? And the apostles said, 'We are the helpers with God'" (lxi., 14; iii., 45).—"O ye who have been given the Books, believe in what we have brought down, for it confirms that which you have with you" (iv., 50).

"And if thou art in doubt of that which we have brought down to thee, ask those who read the Books before thee; because the truth has come to thee from thy Lord, be not of those who are in doubt" (x., 94).—"And those to whom the Books were given did not contradict one another until after knowledge came to them, through their mutual bickering" (iii., 16).—"On that day neither man nor demon[1] shall be asked about his crime" (lv., 39).—"Truly we will question them, one and all, about what they were doing before" (xv., 92-93).—"We have forgotten you as you have forgotten this day" (xxxii., 14; xlv., 33).—"There is nothing hidden from thy Lord" (iii., 4, etc.).[2]—"This is the day in which you may not speak" (lxxvii., 35).—"In the day of Resurrection you will dispute with one another before your Lord" (xxxix., 32).—"On that day we will seal their mouths" (xxxvi., 65).—*And he said further:* "Their tongues shall bear witness against them" (xxiv., 24).—"There is no relationship between *men* on that day nor shall they ask one another anything" (xxiii., 103).—"The day when he shall flee from his brother and his mother and his father" (lxxx., 34-35).—"And they began to question each other" (xxxvii., 27).

"Any of your women who committed adultery, if they raise against them four witnesses about it,—the women such as these are to be kept in houses until death takes them or God shall make for them a dissolution" (iv., 19).—"The adulterer and the adulteress, scourge each of them with a hundred stripes" (xxiv., 2).—"And while he was in the high storey he drew near and hovered, as of the[3] angle of a bow, or nigher still, and he inspired his servant what he inspired him, and will ye dispute with him on what he saw? And he saw him on another descent towards the Garden, near the tree, and the

[1] Translation of *Jinn* which in xv., 27 (see above) has been rendered by "Spirit that dwells in the air."

[2] About this passage see *Foreword*. [3] Length? (doubtful meaning.)

sight swerved not nor wandered" (liii., 7-17).—"And when he came to it he was called from the right side of the valley, in the blessed watery plain, out of the tree, 'O Moses, I am the God of the worlds'" (xxviii., 30).

And Jesus said to the Jews: "I will create for you from clay something in the form of a bird, and I blow thereon, and it shall become a bird by God's command" (iii. 43).—"Naught precluded men from believing when guidance came to them save their saying 'Has God sent a man as His apostle?' say, 'Were there angels on the earth walking in quiet, we had sent them an angel as an apostle'" (xvii., 96-97).—"The good luck of our Lord was raised, because He possesses neither consort nor son" (lxxii., 3).—*And:* "He knows the hidden things, and no one knows the hidden things of His knowledge, save such apostle as is chosen by Him. He sends a guard before him and after him, that he may know that they have delivered the apostleship of their Lord" (lxxii., 26-28).—"Do ye not see how God has created the seven heavens in stories, and has set therein the moon for light" (lxxi., 14).

When God swears, He says thus: "I swear by the Lord of the easts and the wests that I am able" (lxx., 40).—"Bring the unjust and all who follow them and all what they used to serve, and direct them to the way of hell" (xxxvii., 22-23).—"I did not say; if I had said, Thou wouldst have known it, because there is nothing hidden from Thee" (v., 116).—"Then we made *the man* a new creation; blessed be God the best of creators" (xxiii., 14).—"And we have wedded them to wives 'ḥur'ain'" (xliv., 54).—"And we sent to them abundantly fruits and meat such as they like" (lii., 22).—"And round them shall go their sons who resemble beautiful pearls" (lii., 24).

And: "Garden, whose breadth is as the breadth of the heavens and of the earth" (lvii., 21).—"No one understands it but God."[1]—"Righteousness is not that ye turn your faces towards the east or the west, but righteousness is this: that one believes in God and in the last day" (ii., 172).—"Turn thy face towards the east[1] of sacredness; wherever ye be, turn your faces towards it" (ii., 139).—"God's are the easts and the wests; and towards whatever directions you

[1] See *Foreword.*

turn your faces, there is the face of God, because God is broad and knowing" (ii., 109).—"If all men gathered together from the East as far as the West to change one letter from the words of God, they will not be able (to do it)."[1]

"Is it thou who didst say to men, 'Know me and my mother as two gods, and serve us instead of God'" (v., 116).—*From the Sūrah of the "Spider":* "Do not dispute with the holders of the Books except with the nicest of words" (xxix., 45).—"Do good works because God loves those who do good works" (v., 94).—"And they say, 'We will not believe in thee until He make a fountain gush forth for thee from the earth; or there be made for thee a garden of palms and grapes, and thou make rivers flow round it; or thou make heaven to fall as thou saidst; or thou bring us God or receiving angels; or there be made for thee a house of gold; or thou climb up into the heaven. And we will not believe in thee until thou bring down to us a book from heaven that we may read.' Say to them, 'Praise be to my Lord! am I anything but a man messenger?[2] What precluded men from believing when guidance came to them . . ." (xvii., 92-96).—"Say *to them*, *God* is a sufficient witness between me and you that I am His messenger to you" (cf. xi., 2; xiii., 43; xlvi., 7 and 8).—"And when they see a sign they doubt and say, 'This is obvious sorcery'" (xxxvii., 14).[3]

"Mary, daughter of 'Amram, who guarded her private parts, and we breathed therein of our spirit, and she verified the words of her Lord and his Book and was of the devout" (lxvi., 12).—"O sister of Aaron, thy father was not a bad man, nor thy mother a blasphemer" (xix., 29).—"The heavens *are* rolled up in His right hand" (xxxix., 67).—*And* "the hands *of God* are outspread" (v., 69).—*And* "the hands of God are above their hands" (xlviii., 10).—"And heaven—we have built it with hands" (li., 47).—*And* "the good luck of the Lord is high" (lxxii., 3).—*And* "He is

[1] See *Foreword*. [2] Or: apostle.

[3] Between this verse and the next is a large heading "Prayer of the Muslims" which is: "O God, pray over Muḥammad and over the children of his paternal uncle, and bless Muḥammad and the children of his paternal uncle, as Thou hast prayed over, and blessed, and hadst mercy upon Abraham and the children of his paternal uncle; for He is high and glorious."

sitting on a throne."[1]—*And* "He ascended to heaven while it was but smoke" (xli., 10).

"I do not swear by this land, and thou dwellest in this land; and the Father and the one who is begotten of Him. We have created man in anger"[2] (xc., 1-4).—"The Holy Spirit brought down from the Lord grace and light."[3]—*And* "God said. 'O Jesus,[4] son of Mary, remember my grace towards thee and towards thy mother, when I fortified thee with the Holy Spirit'" (v., 109).—"Are unbelievers who say 'God is the third of three," (v., 77).—"Of the holders of the Books there is a nation, *that is to say a community*, who stand all the night and recite the miracles of God; and they adore, and believe in, God, and in the last day, and bid good things and forbid bad things, and do charitable things with ease; and they are righteous" (iii., 109-110).

"The Jews said, 'God's hands are fettered'; the hands of Jews are fettered, and they are cursed for what they said" (v., 69).—"*The Jews*' disbelief in God's signs, and their killing of the prophets undeservedly, and their saying, that *their* hearts are uncircumcised,—nay, (God) has stamped their unbelief on their *hearts*" (iv., 154).—"And thou wilt find the nearest in love to those who have believed to be those who say, 'We are Christians'; and among them there are priests and monks, and they will not be proud" (v., 85).—"There is nothing that is moist nor aught that is dry which is not known in this Book" (vi., 59).—"Even the weight of a grain of mustard does not escape from thy Lord, in heavens and in earth; and there is nothing, small or great, that is not known in this Book" (xxxiv., 3).—"And if thou art in doubt of that which we have brought down unto thee, ask those who read the Books before thee" (x., 94).

"A garden whose breadth is as the breadth of the heavens and the earth" (lvii., 21; iii., 127).—"In it are rivers of water without corruption, and rivers of milk the taste whereof has not changed, and rivers of wine delicious and pleasing to those who drink it, and rivers of honey clarified, and there they have of all fruits" (xlvii., 16-17).—"Eat and drink with pleasure for that which you have done; and reclining on couches, *that is to say* '*takhthā*,'[5] which are put in rows; and

[1] See *Foreword.* [2] Lit. liver. [3] See *Foreword.*

[4] Here also spelt '*Īsa* and not *Īshō*'.

[5] A Persian word in the Persian plural form meaning "couches."

we have wedded them to wives 'ḥur'ain'" (lii., 19-20).—"And we have abundantly sent them fruits and meat such as they like" (lii., 22).—"And round them shall go their boys who resemble beautiful pearls" (lii., 24).

"And for him who fears the standing up before his Lord are gardens twain in which there are two flowing springs in which there are two pairs of every fruit" (lv., 46-52).—"In them are women beautiful in sight, whom no corporeal nor spiritual being has approached" (lv., 56).—*And there in the Garden:* "fruits such as they choose, and meat of fowl as they desire and women 'ḥur'ain' who resemble beautiful pearls" (lvi., 20-22).—"The righteous shall drink *in the Garden* of a cup the mixture of which is Kafru [1] (lxxvi., 5).—"And flagons of silver made with symmetry; and they shall be given to drink in the *Garden* a cup the mixture of which is Zangibla; [2] and there is in it a spring called Salibasīla; [3] and there shall go round them boys continually; and when thou seest them thou wilt think them scattered pearls" (lxxvi., 16-20).—"Praise be to the One who hath made good His promise to us, and hath given us the earth as inheritance; for we dwell in the Garden wherever we please" (xxxix., 74).

Our Dissertation against the Arabs, i.e. *Muslims, has extended as far as here. We have refuted their objection concerning the Trinity and the Incarnation of the Son, and by proofs taken from nature and from philosophical books we have demonstrated our truth; then we have confuted them in many points from their own book; after that we have arranged in one systematic division parts of the Ḳur'ān, which has been translated from their language into Syriac, and we have shortly refuted it in the column that is below it; because in the previous chapters we have given a detailed refutation. The time has now come to put an end to our labour. Let any one who reads and understands, profits and makes others profit, pray for Mar Dionysius the stranger, who is Jacob Barṣalībi of Milīṭīni, Metropolitan of Amed.*

[1] The *Kāfūr* (Camphor) of our Ḳur'āns, the right meaning of which no one has ever understood. See Tabari, *Tafsīr*, xxix., 128.

[2] The *Zanjabil* of our Ḳur'āns, generally translated by "ginger."

[3] The *Salsabīl* of our Ḳur'āns.

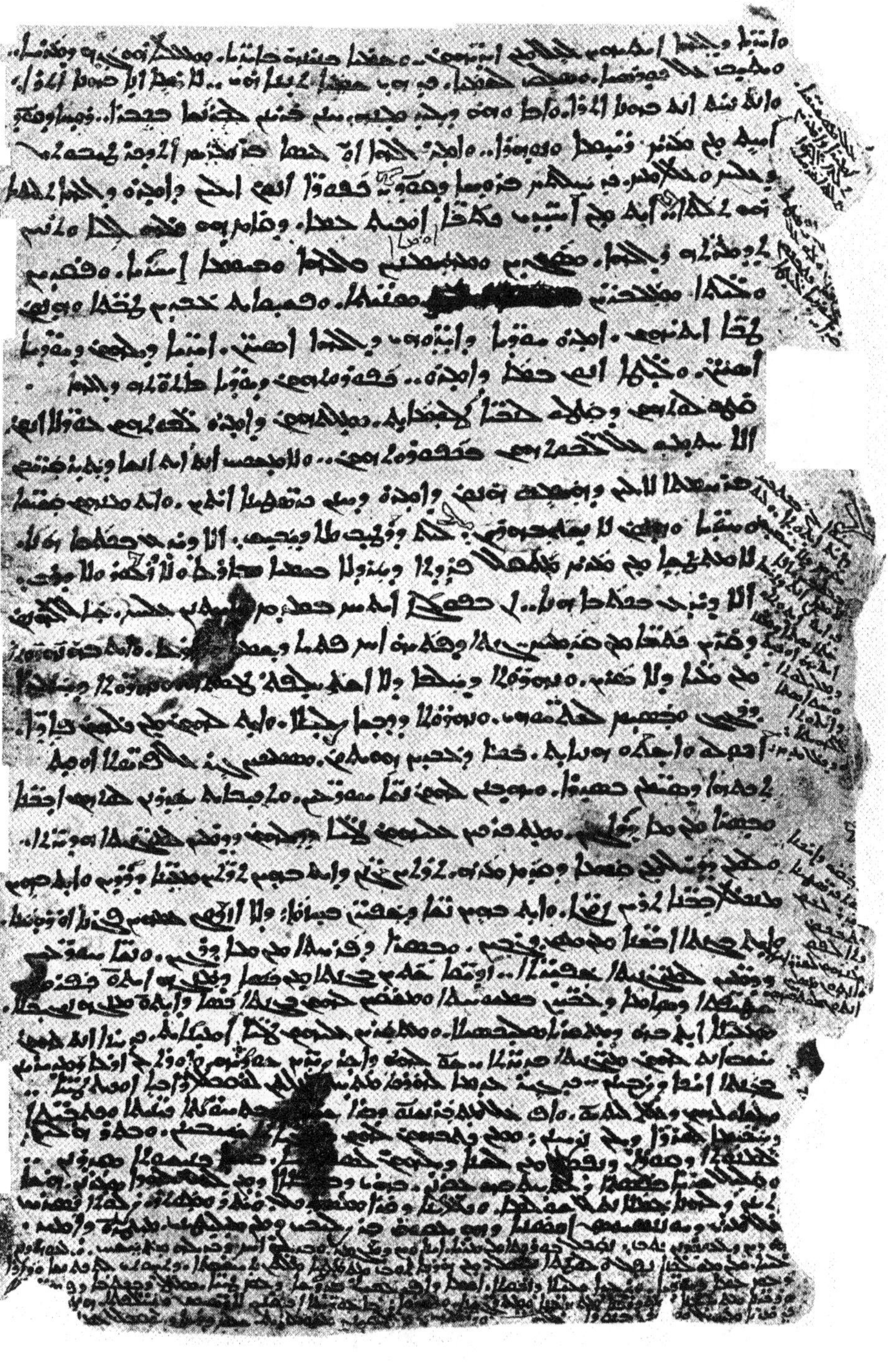

Syriac MS. Ḳur'ān, Fol. 84*b*

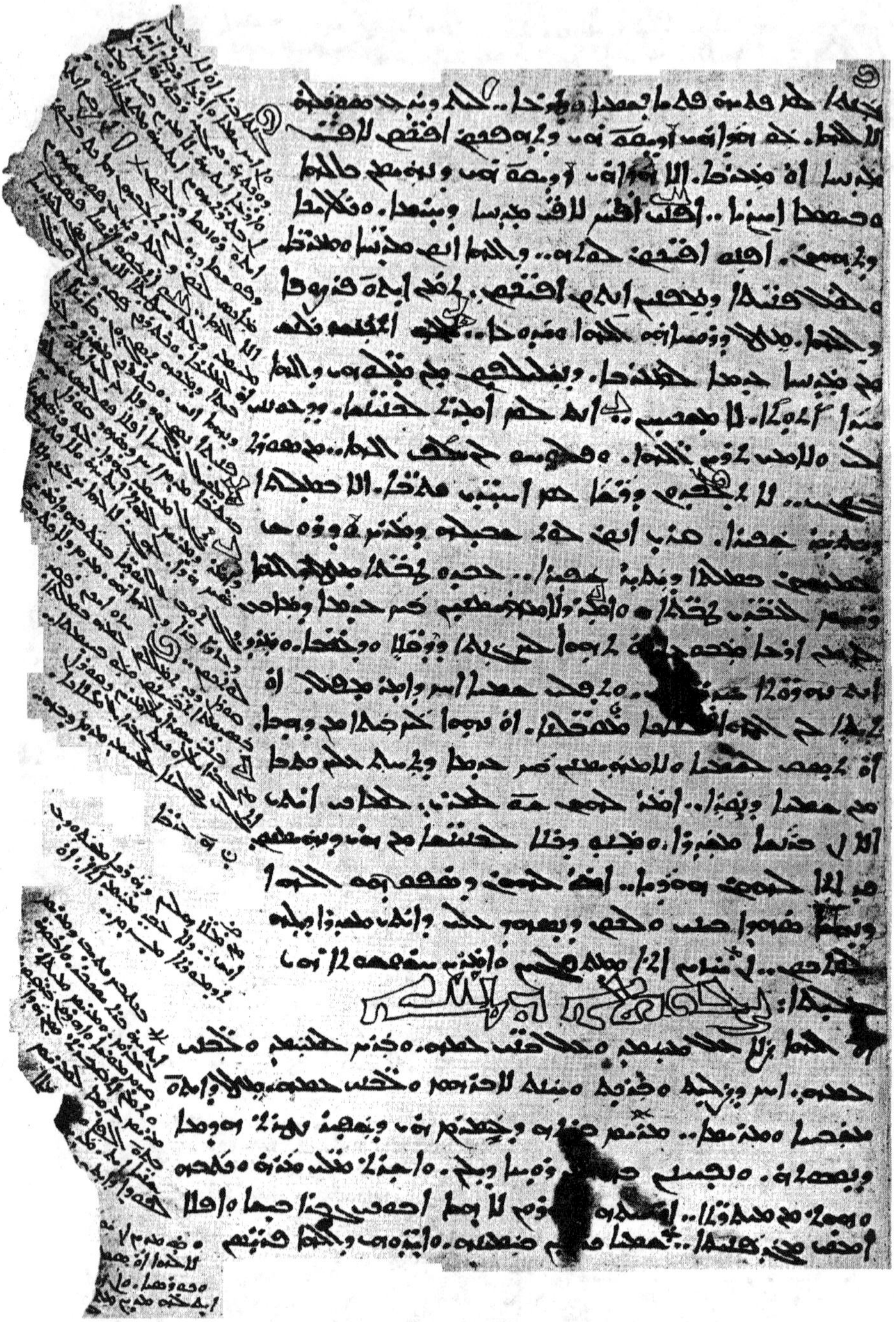

Syriac MS. Ḳur'ān, Fol. 84*a*

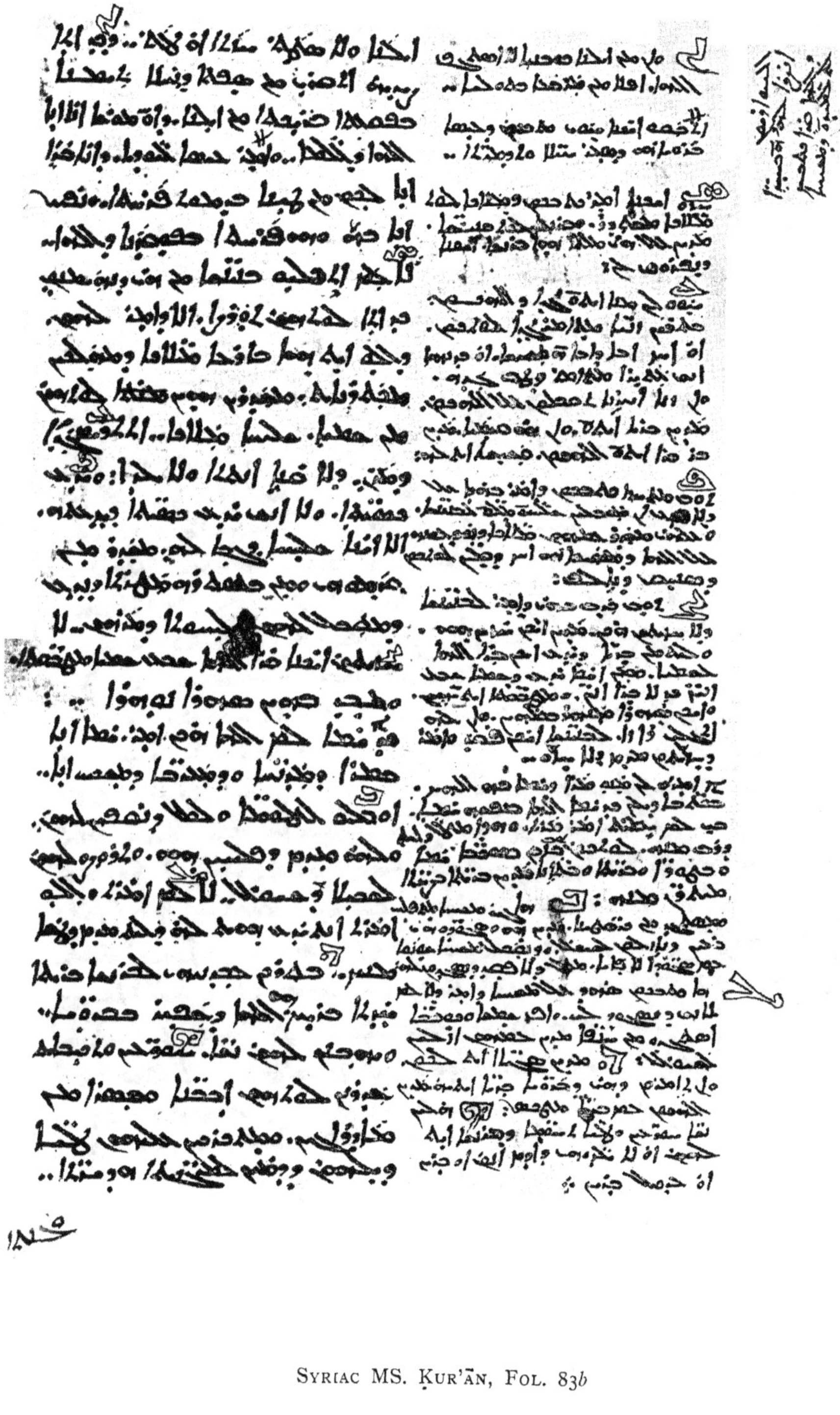

Syriac MS. Ḳur'ān, Fol. 83*b*

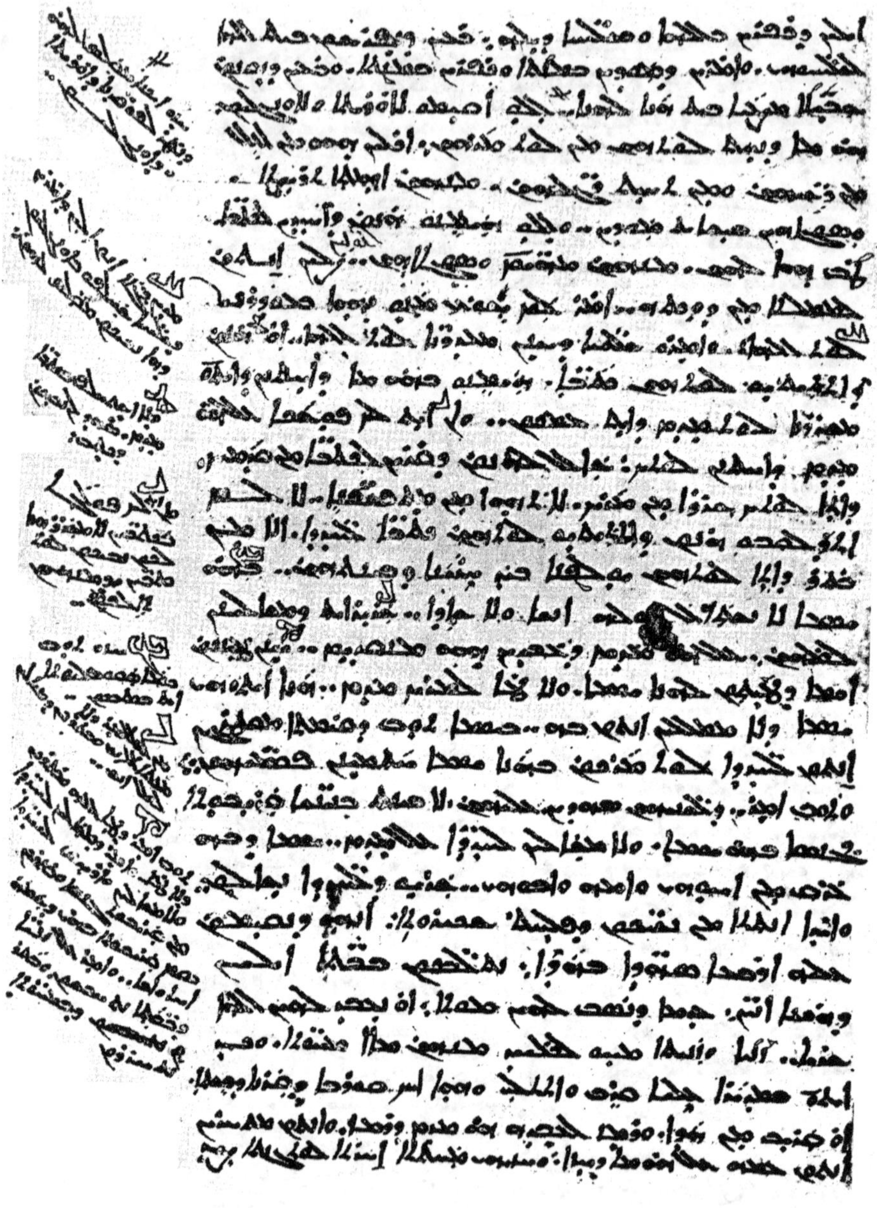

Syriac MS. Ḳur'ān, Fol. 83*a*

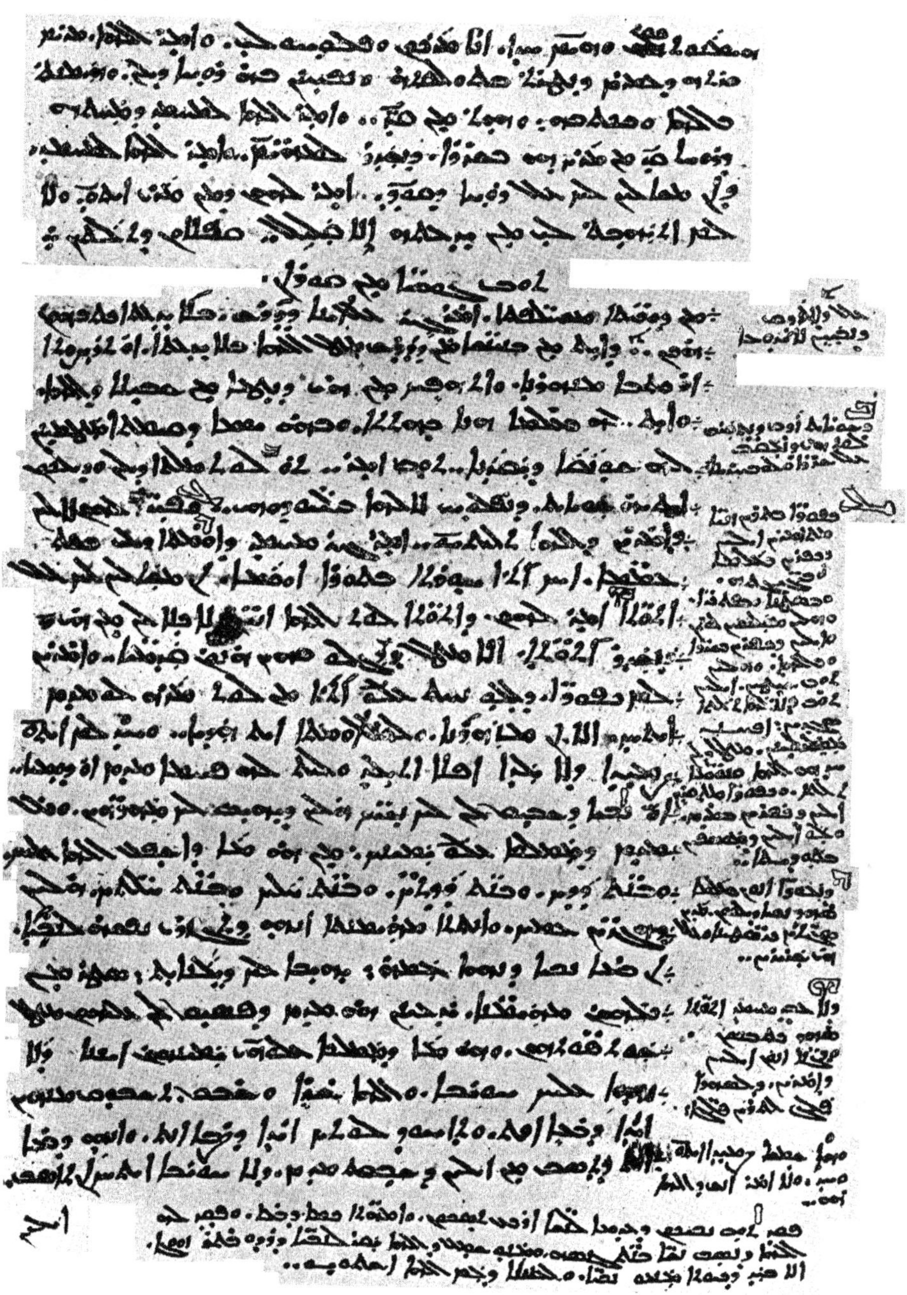

Syriac MS. Ḳur'ān, Fol. 82*b*

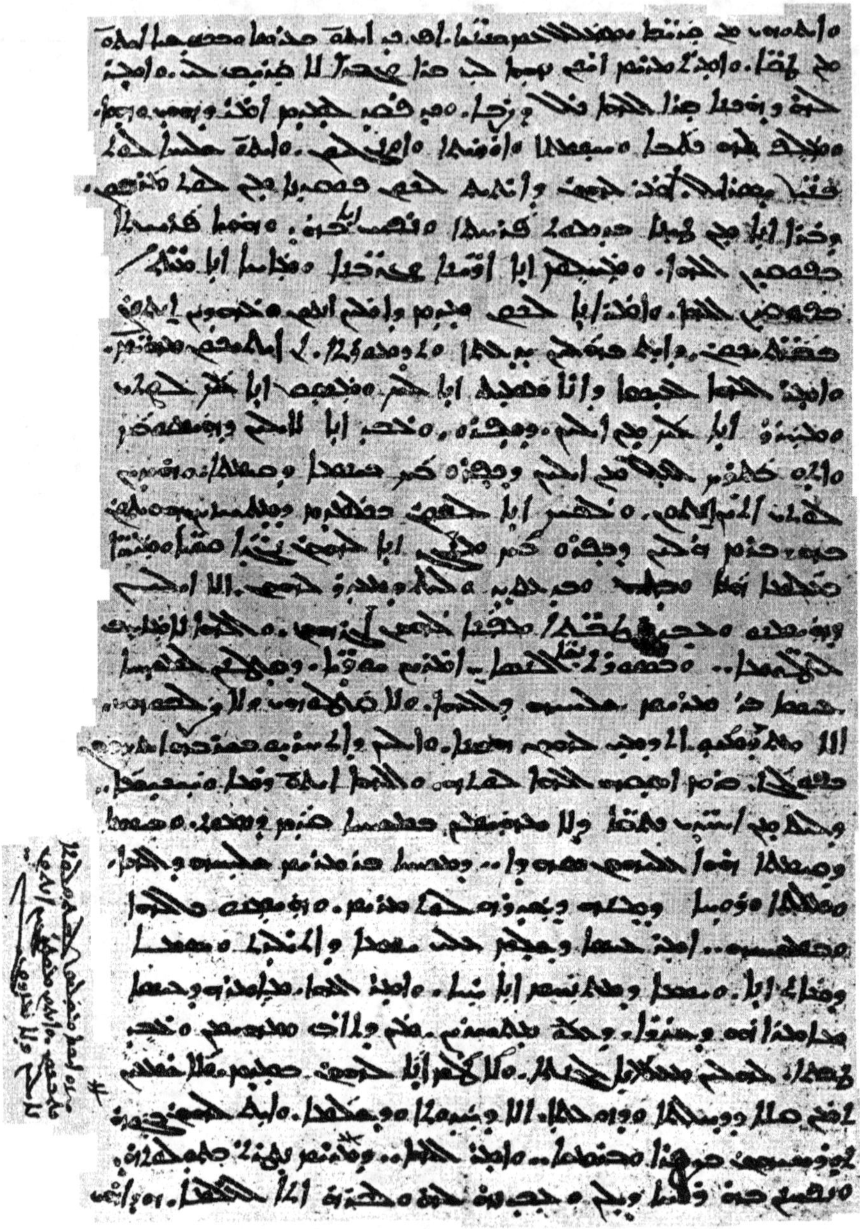

Syriac MS. Ḳur'ān, Fol. 82*a*

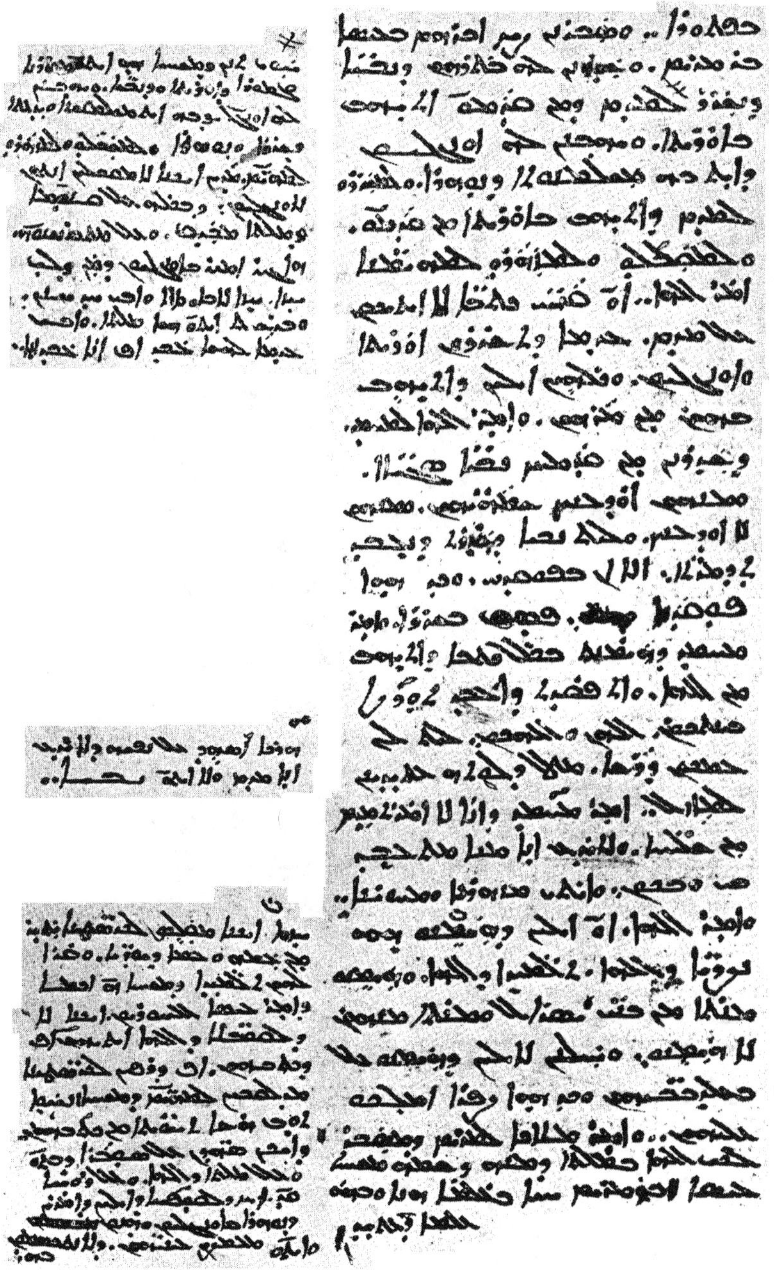

SYRIAC MS. ḲUR'ĀN, FOL. 81*b*

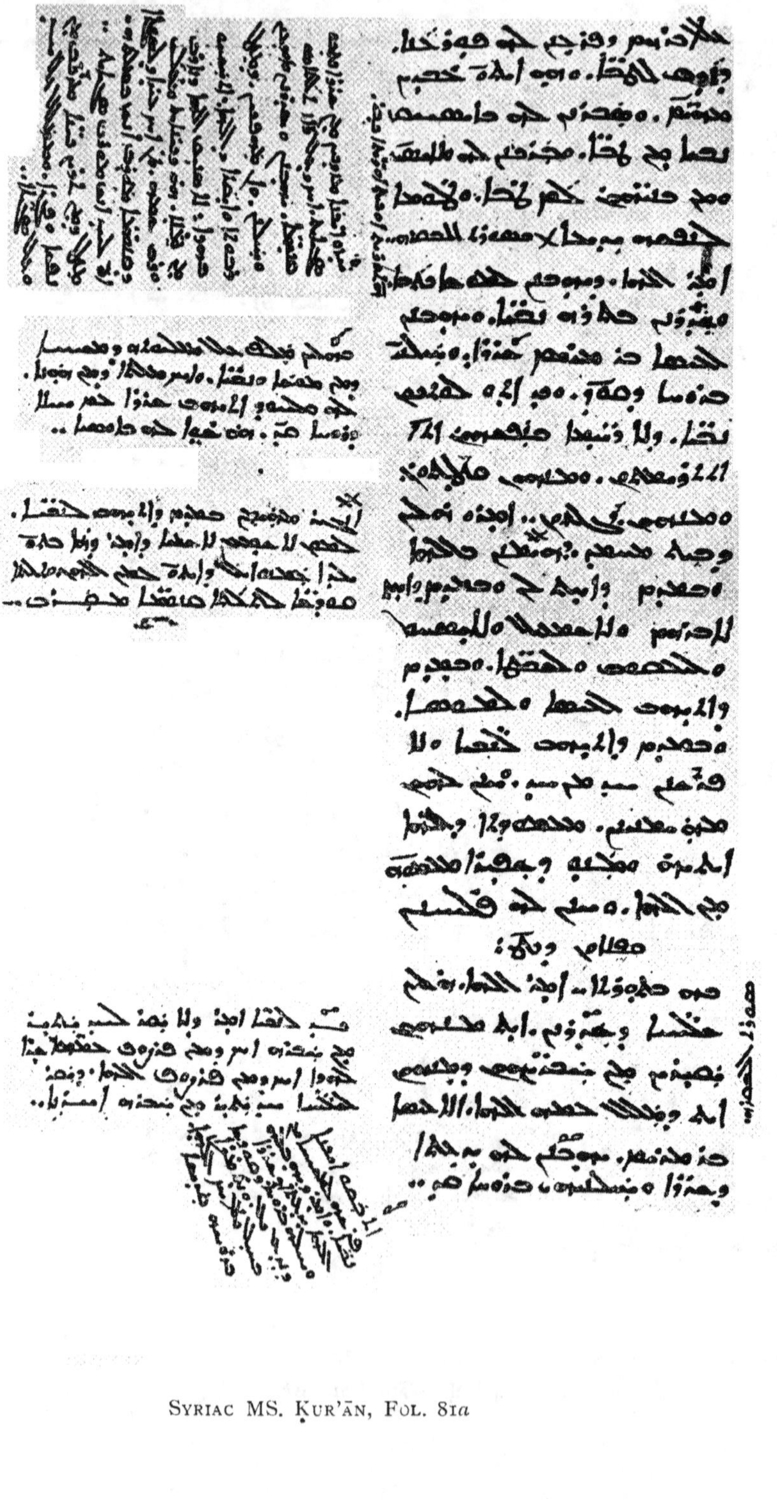

Syriac MS. Ḳur'ān, Fol. 81*a*

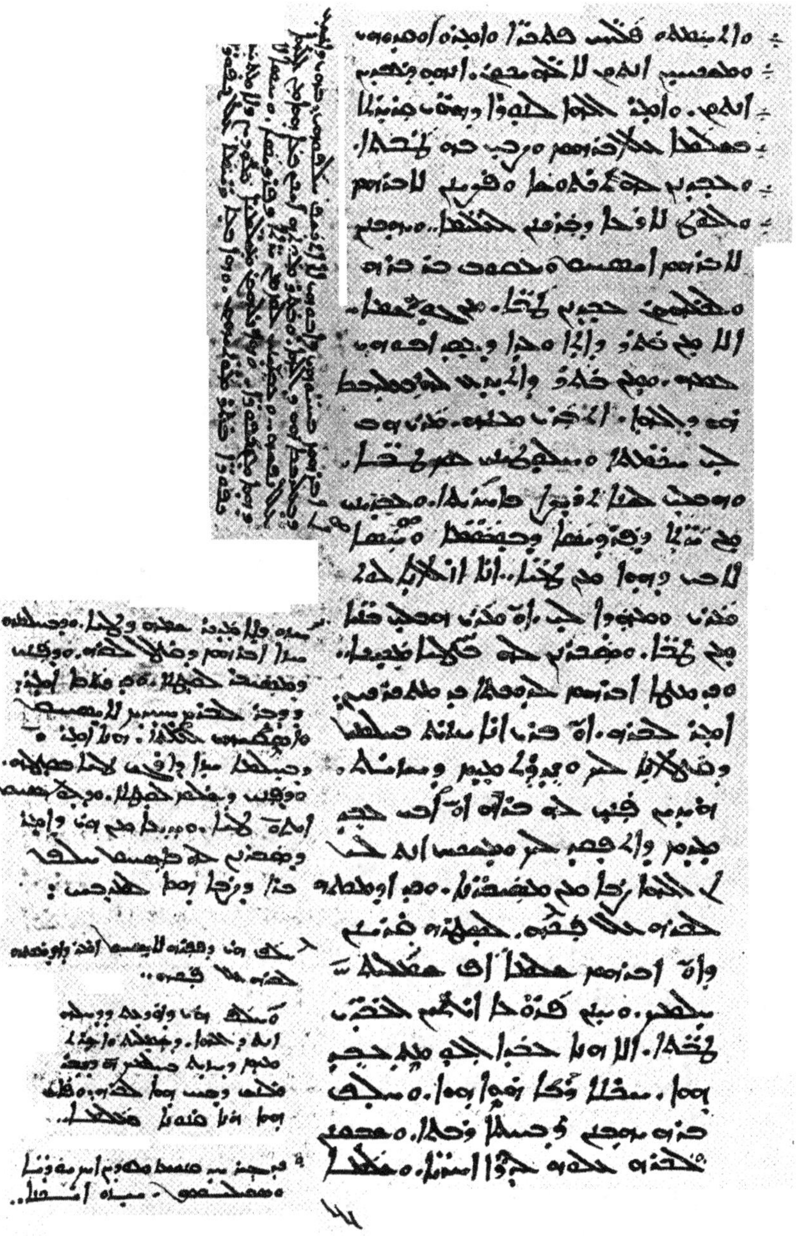

Syriac MS. Ḳur'ān, Fol. 80*b*

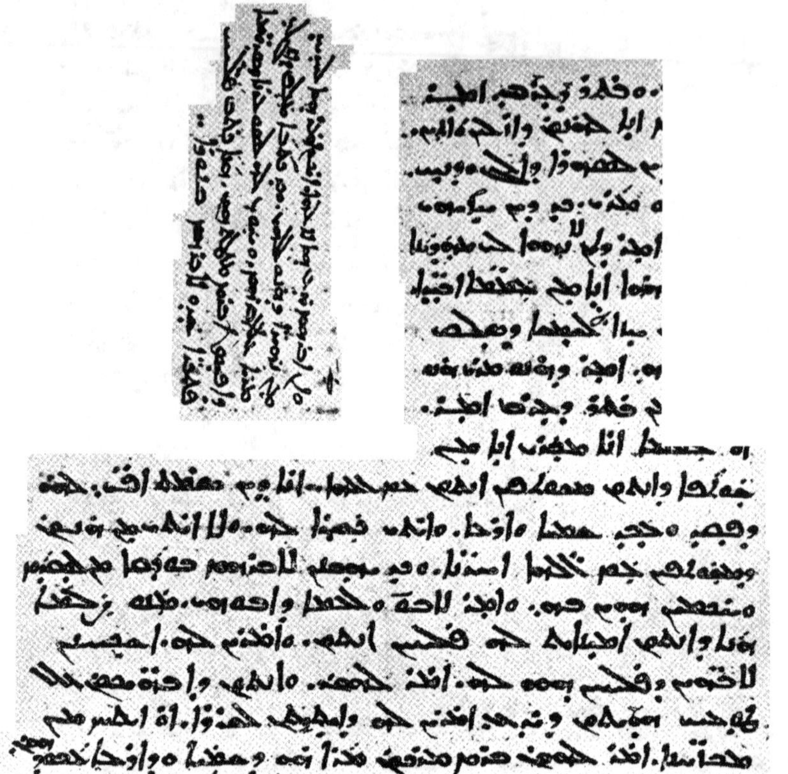

Syriac MS. Ḳur'ān, Fol. 80*a*

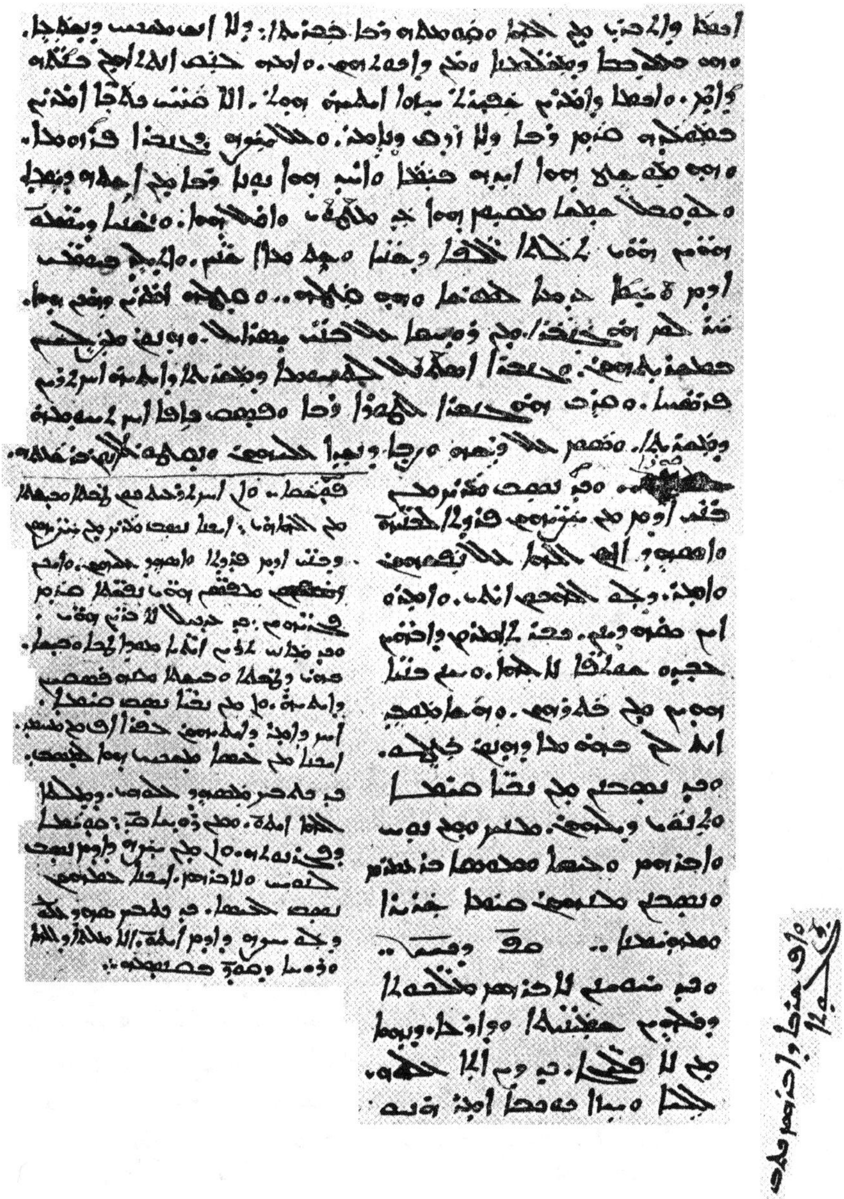

Syriac MS. Ḳur'ān, Fol. 79*b*

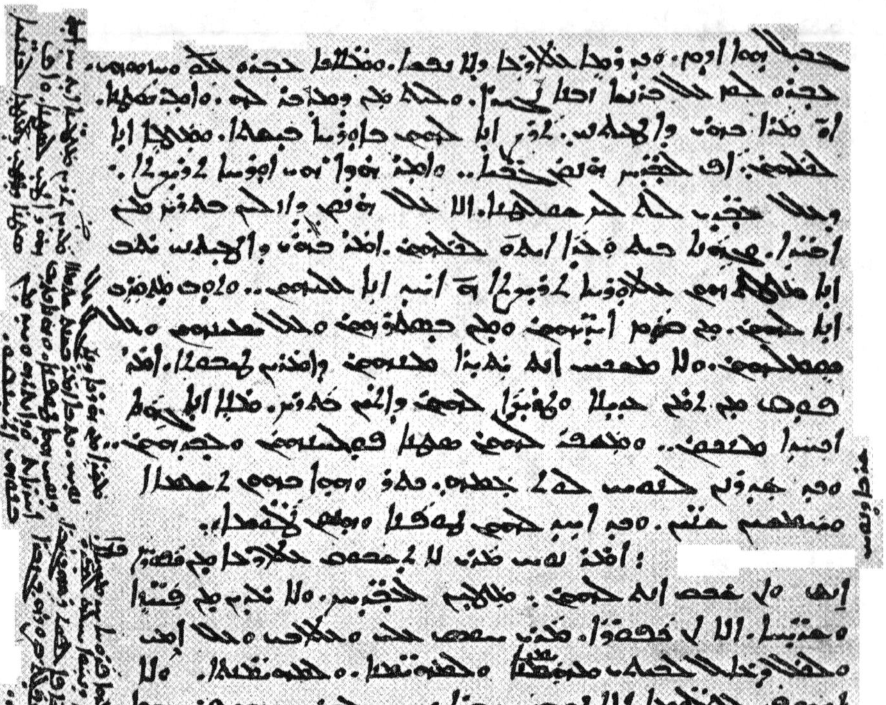

Syriac MS. Ḳur'ān, Fol. 79a

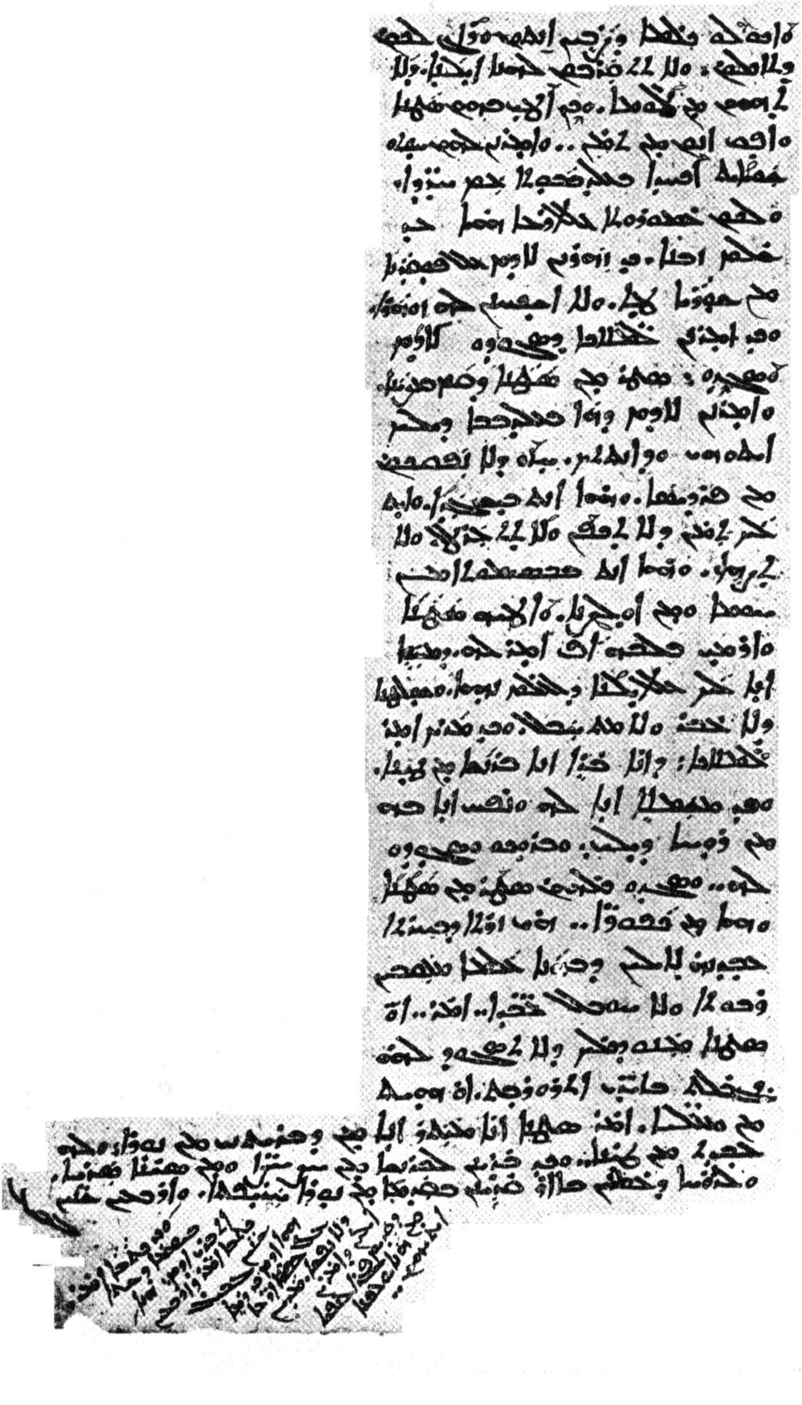

Syriac MS. Ḳur'ān, Fol. 78*b*

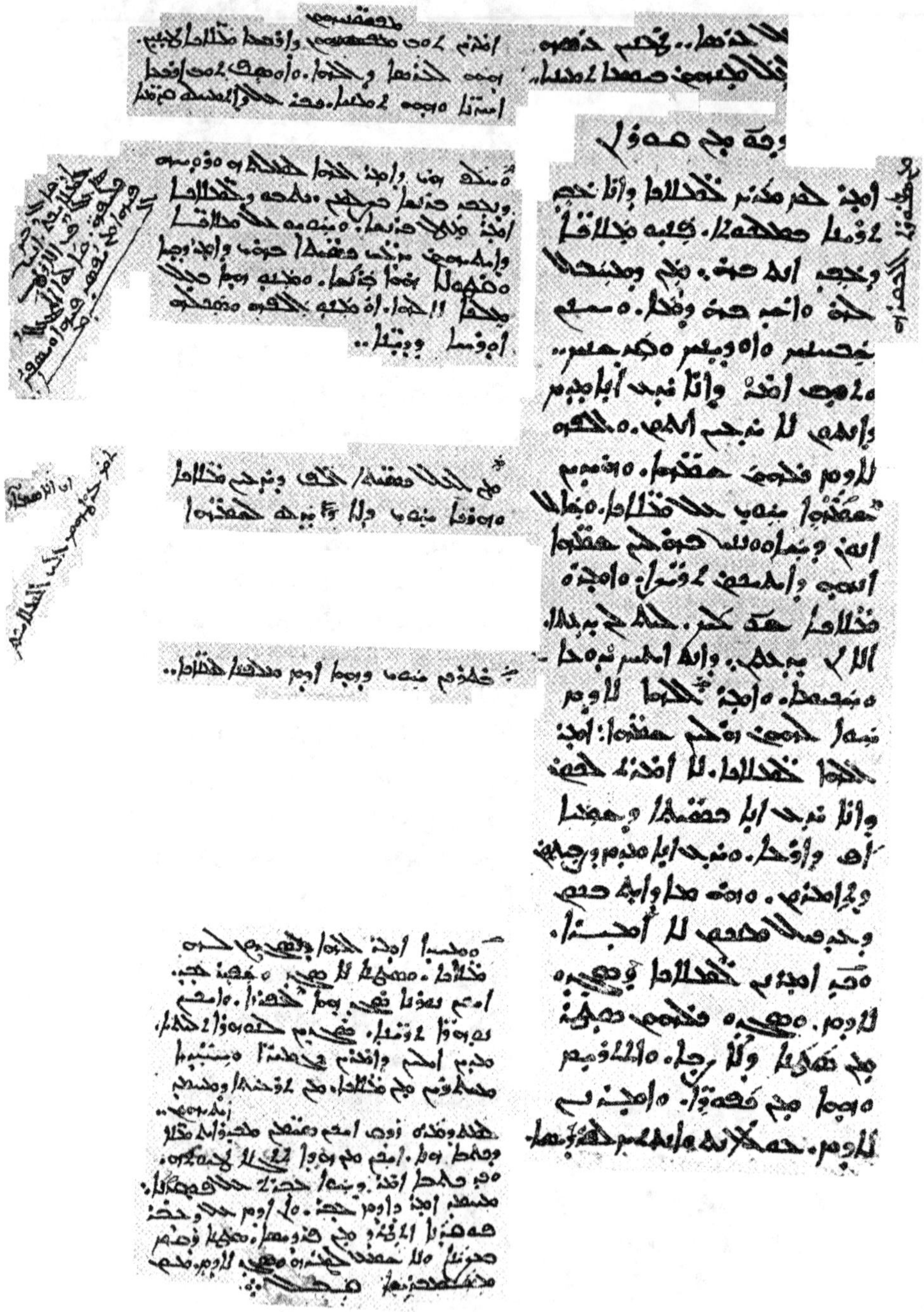

Syriac MS. Ḳur'ān, Fol. 78*a*

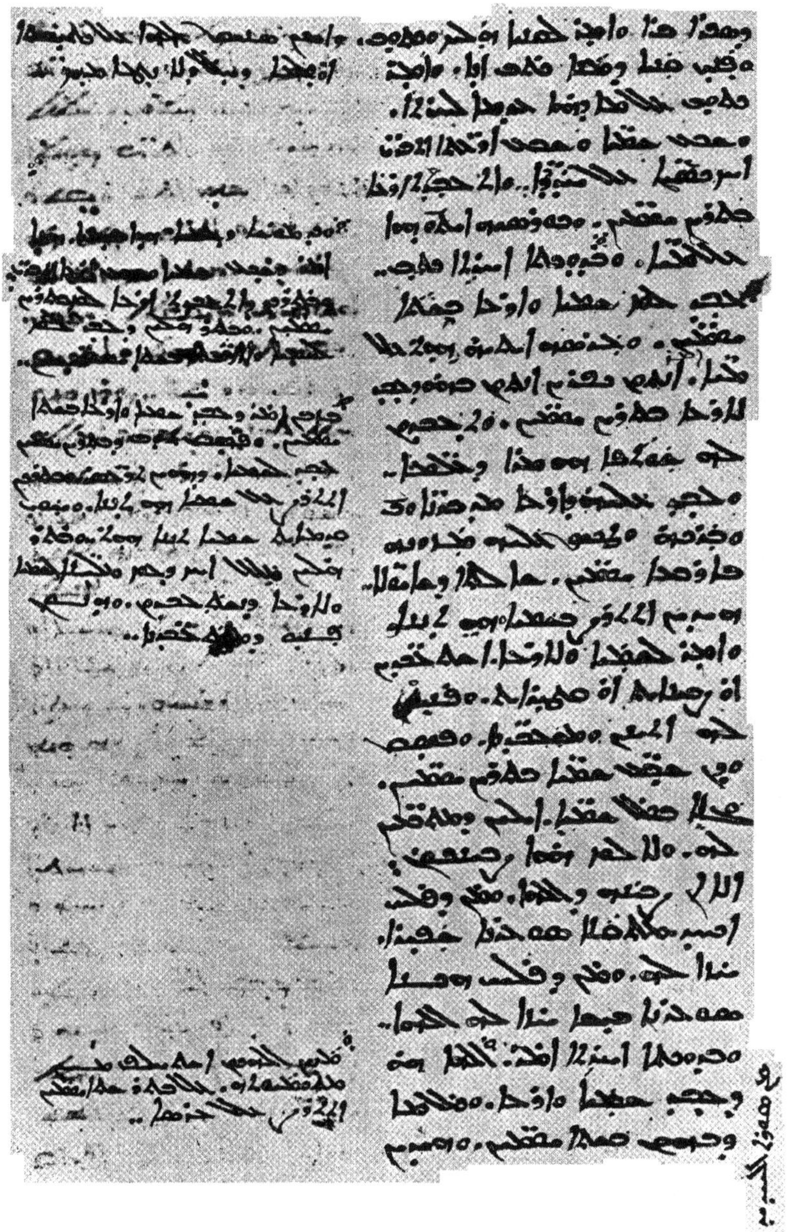

Syriac MS. Ḳur'ān, Fol. 77b

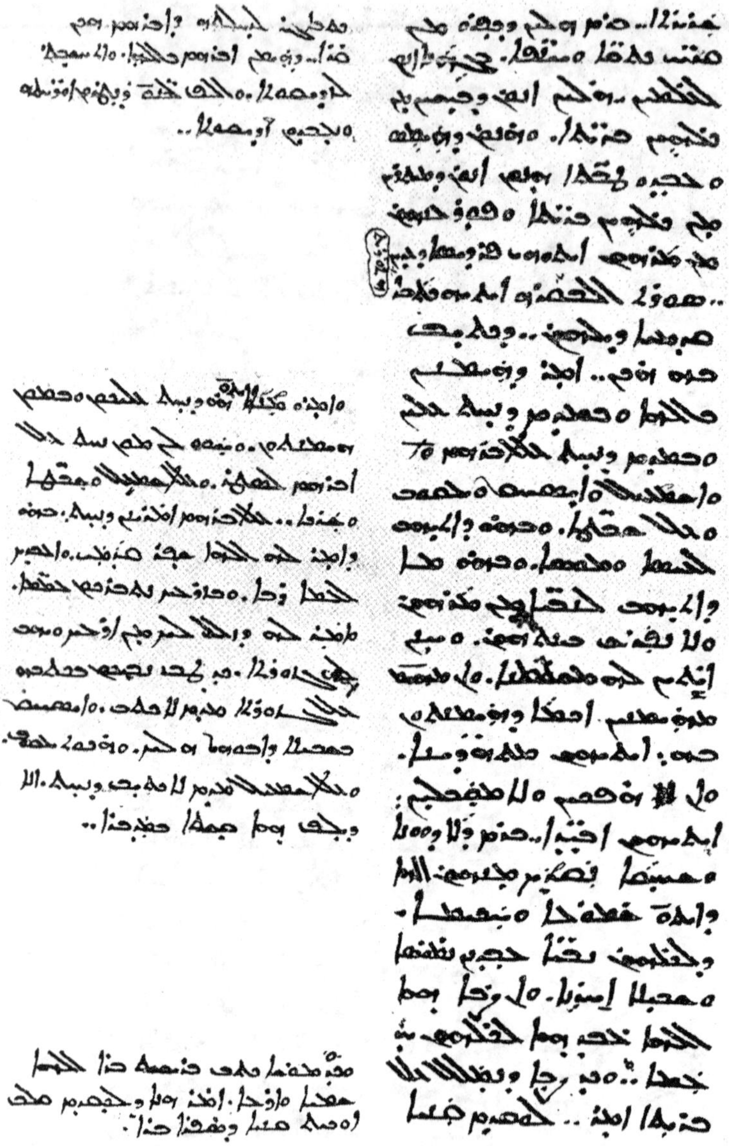

Syriac MS. Ḳur'ān, Fol. 77*a*

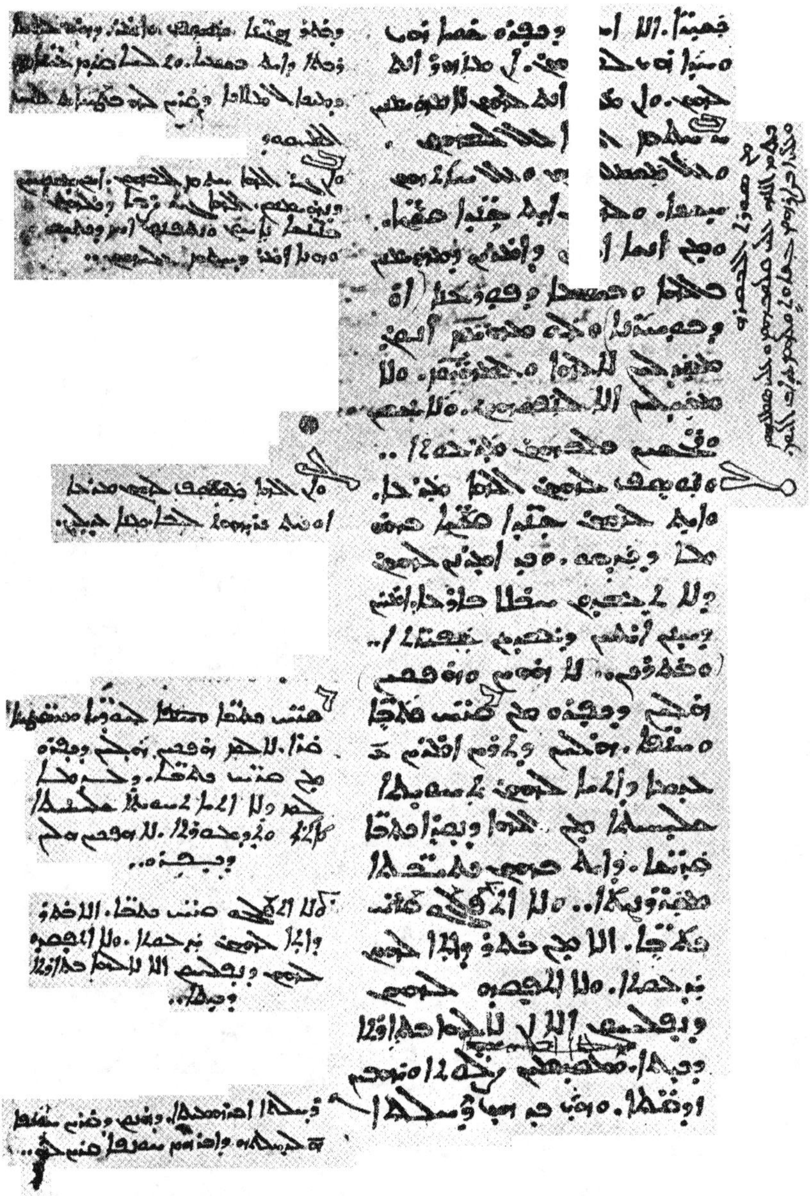

Syriac MS. Ḳur'ān, Fol. 76*b*

SYRIAC MS. ḲUR'ĀN, FOL. 76*a*

SUPPLEMENTARY NOTE.

While the above pages were in the press, the authorities of Harvard University—to whom I here take the liberty to tender my sincerest thanks—were so kind as to place at my disposal, through the intermediary of my friend Dr. Rendel Harris, a manuscript described as "Harvard University Semitic Museum N°. 4019," and containing all the controversial works of Barṣalībi mentioned by Baumstark in his *Geschichte der Syrischen Literatur* (p. 297). This MS. formerly belonged to Dr. R. Harris in whose collection it was numbered 83. On fol. 47b we are informed that it was transcribed in Mardin, Saturday, 14th March, 1898, by the priest Gabriel, from a MS. dated 1813 of the Greeks (A.D. 1502) and written in the monastery of Mar Abel and Mar Abraham, near Midyād, in Ṭur 'Abdīn. So far as our present study is concerned we venture to make the following remarks :[1]

A

The Harvard MS. exhibits all the errors of the copyist of our MS. to which we have drawn attention (with the exception of the grammatical slip in Ḳur'ān iv., 9 and *imart* in xvii., 94), and we do not deem it useful to repeat them here, but we will tabulate the fresh mistakes into which the copyist of the Harvard MS. has fallen, and which the copyist of our MS. was shrewd enough to avoid :

(*a*) In Ḳur'ān i., 7 read ܘܠܐ for ܘܟܠ (fol. 48a and possibly also our MS. *primâ manu*). (*b*) In ii., 3 the letter *hé*, which stood in the original MS. as an abbreviation for ܗܝܡܢܘ has been wrongly read as the pronoun ܗܘܢ and erroneously added to the preceding word which has thus become ܘܬܫܡܠܐܗܘܢ (fol. 48b). (*c*) In xli., 10 read ܘܗܝ for ܘܗܘ (fol. 49b). (*d*) In xli., 10 read ܘܦܫܘ for ܘܦܫܡ (fol. 49b). (*e*) In xlii., 11 read ܘܢܟܠ for ܘܢܟܐ (fol. 49b). (*f*) In xxi., 56 read ܠܗ for ܠܗܒܐ (fol. 53a). (*g*) In xxi., 57 read ܒܕܡ for ܐܒܕܡ fol. 53a). (*h*) In xxi., 71 read ܐܠܐܪܥܐ for ܠܐܪܥܐ (fol. 53a). (*i*) In xxi., 72 read ܒܕ ܒܕܡܗ for ܒܕܒܗ

[1] We take the Syriac words that follow in the order in which they occur in the text. The references are to the Harvard MS.

(fol. 53[b]). (*j*) In iii., 43 read ܕܟܠܬܒ̈ܟܘܢ for ܕܟܠܬ̈ܢܟܘܢ (fol. 55[a]). (*k*) In x, 94 read ܠܟ for ܠܢ (fol. 56[b]). (*l*) In liii., 9 read ܡܘܕܥܬ for ܡܘܕܥܬܐ (fol. 57[a]). (*m*) In xxviii. 30 possibly read ܕܝܡܝܢܬܐ for ܬܝܡܢܬܐ (fol. 57[a]) and ܬܝܡܢܬܐ of our MS., but this may possibly be due to the fact that the Ḳur'ān might have read التيمن for الايمن. (*n*) In lxii., 12 read ܕܢܟܦܘܬܗ̇ for ܕܢܦܩܘܬܗ̇ (fol. 58[b]). (*o*) In lxxvi., 17 read ܠܗܘܢ for ܠܗܘܡ (fol. 59[b]).

B

On the other hand the Harvard MS. contains readings which tend to improve both the text and the translation of our MS. In the translation given above we have taken account of all these improvements for the benefit of the English reader. Two such readings are mentioned under A ; the others are :

(*a*) In Ḳur'ān xx., 114 before the word *Zuhhāra* the particle ܡܢ (fol. 50[b]) is missing in our MS. (*b*) In xxxviii., 77 for ܡܢܗ (fol. 51[a]) our MS. reads erroneously ܡܢ. (*c*) In the traditional verse about Adam the Harvard MS. (fol. 51[a]) has ܚܒ for our ܘܚܒ. (*d*) In xxiii., 103 our MS. omits after *Lā* the verb ܗܘܐ (fol. 56[b]). (*e*) In iii., 43 the verb ܘܗܘܐ (fol. 57[a]) corrects our pronoun ܘܗܘ. (*f*) In xvii., 96 the copyist of our MS. has by homoioteleuton omitted after ܕܐܡܪ the following sentence :

ܒܪܢܫܐ ܫܠܝܚܐ ܕܝܠܗ ܘܐܡܪ ܕܫܕܪ ܐܠܗܐ

"(. . . said), Has God sent a man as His apostle ? And he said" (*sic*) . . . (fol. 57[a].) The *wāw* before the verb *imar* seems to be erroneous.

C

Some other lexicographical and grammatical features worth mentioning are : (*a*) the word ܦܨܦܨܬܐ is used in Harvard (fol. 56[b]) concerning iii., 106, while our MS. has (apparently by a later hand) ܢܘܠܡ The first reading seems to be a wrong transliteration of the

Arabic الفاسقون which has been rendered into '*awālīn* (the reading of our MS.) by an owner or a copyist, and possibly not by the first translator himself, unless the word were to be ܦܣܝܩ̈ܐ "the cut off, or rejected ones." (*b*) In iv., 19 Harvard has ܕܒܩܘܣܩܘܢ (fol. 57[a]) and our MS. ܕܒܩܣܩܘܢ. (*c*) Both MSS. have the erroneous readings ܣܓܕ̈ܘܗܘܢ for ܣܓܕ̈ܝܢ in xvii., 93, and ܟܒܕ̈ܬܐ (fol. 58[b]) for ܟܒܕܬܐ in xc., 4.

D

The Garshūni words and phrases taken from the text of the Ḳur'ān and written mostly on the margins of our MS. are absent in the Harvard copy. This bears out the opinion that we expressed concerning their origin: that they were due to some owners or late copyists.

E

The first half of the story of 'Auṣ or 'Auj b. A'naḳ is in the Harvard MS. also (fol. 52[a]) written in the first column, and the second half in the second column. Evidently the blunder goes back to a very early MS., and it is even possible that it is due to Barṣalībi himself, who discovered it in time and promptly corrected it. What seems to render this view possible is the fact that both MSS. break the sentence with the same word, and that the heading: "Ḳur'ān" is written in both of them in the body of the text immediately after the part of the story told in the first column, in order to show that it is not to be taken as Ḳur'ānic. The story forms a part of the didactic side of the work of Barṣalībi, like the first long note found in the second column of the first page. See Facsimile.

F

Leaves 4[b]-6[a] of the Harvard MS. contain an Index of the contents of all three discourses of Barṣalībi against the Muslims. On fol. 5[b] the third discourse is introduced in this Index as follows: "Third discourse against the Muslims, containing various parts of the Ḳur'ān in the first column, with their refutation in the second column." Our MS. is deficient here, and some leaves have disappeared from it which probably contained this Index with the above statement.

www.ingramcontent.com/pod-product-compliance
Lightning Source LLC
Chambersburg PA
CBHW051800230426
43670CB00012B/2373